THE MOST AMAZING
FOR YOUN(

15

AMAZING & INSPIRING
TRUE TALES

FROM BASEBALL'S GREATEST BATTERS

TERRENCE ARMSTRONG

CONTENTS

INTRODUCTION
BATTER'S UP!

Anyone who has ever swung a bat and connected it with an oncoming baseball knows just how incredible it feels—how exhilarating it is to see that ball soar into the air as outfielders scramble to catch it and runners make their way to base.

This is an exhilaration that the 15 baseball batters discussed in this book all know very well. From Pete Rose and Jose Canseco to Manny Ramirez and Mookie Betts, all of the players presented here are guys who truly love the game.

Some of them, like Alex Rodriguez (better known as A-Rod), started playing ball at an incredibly young age. Alex was only 18 when he first made his debut in Major League Baseball. Others, with their undying love of baseball, have demonstrated an incredibly long shelf life, playing well into their 40s. Pete Rose played until he was 45!

None of these baseball players are perfect—they certainly had their ups and downs, both in the game of baseball and the game of life. But they did their best and learned plenty of valuable lessons along the way.

This book explores not just the raw stats and game-winning records of these baseball greats, but also the *life-winning* qualities they demonstrated during their careers, for they were all MVPs in more ways than one. Read on to learn more about what made these baseball batters so great!

JOSE CANSECO
THE GOAL-SETTER

In the late 1980s, Jose Canseco was a rising star. In 1985, he had swiftly advanced through the Minor League system, from Double-A to Triple-A. During that blockbuster season, Jose was named the Minor League Baseball Player of the Year.

The Big Leagues took notice of his effort, and that September Jose Canseco ended up on the roster of the Oakland Athletics. By 1998, he was Major League Baseball's MVP. The 24-year-old hit 40 home runs and stole 40 bases that season, setting a record that no one thought would ever exist.

Interestingly, Jose set this unique goal for himself at the start of the 1988 season. He openly announced it was his intention to hit 40 homers and steal 40 bases. Some might have thought that Jose was setting himself up for failure. After all, he had set a high bar for himself, one that many critics didn't think it was possible to reach.

But Jose Canseco didn't fail. From a young age, he had been determined to reach any goal he set—not because life was easy, but because it could often be so hard.

Canseco was born in communist Cuba in 1964, when the country was being controlled by the hardline dictator Fidel Castro. Castro's Cuba was not the friendliest place when it came to individual initiative and free enterprise. First of all, Castro nationalized everything on the island in order to stifle American interests. Castro then decided to unilaterally ban professional sports.

Such an approach wasn't good for baseball, and it wasn't good for business. This was something Jose Canseco's father quickly realized, as the policies of the communists began to cut into the bottom line of the oil company where he was an executive. For this reason, Canseco's family was looking for an escape from Cuba as soon as possible.

Their window of opportunity arrived in 1965. Jose Canseco and his parents made their way north to Miami, Florida. It was here that Jose Canseco first developed his life-long passion for baseball. He set early goals to improve his athletic ability, and by the time he was in high school, he had become a standout star.

His father had once again become a successful businessman. He had fully adjusted to life in Miami and provided his son with further incentive to excel at his chosen sport. Jose Canseco's dad actually offered him $5 for every home run he hit! The fact that his father was willing to reward him for reaching an objective helped to instill a sense of goal-setting in the young man.

Shortly after Jose Canseco graduated from high school, he was drafted by the Oakland Athletics. As previously mentioned, Jose worked his way through the Oakland A's Minor League farm teams, rapidly rising to Double-A and then Triple-A status. One of his early mentors was a Minor League coach by the name of Dennis Rogers, who instilled in him the need to "hustle." Although he understood Jose's potential, Rogers also identified situations where he wasn't making the most of it.

During one game, Jose hit a pop-up ball that was launched so high it seemed as if it would never come back down. This was not a home run, but since it took so long for the opposing team to get the ball, Jose should have had plenty of enough time to get to second or maybe even third base. Rogers was dismayed, however, to see Jose stop at first base.

Dennis Rogers later took Jose Canseco aside and lectured him about how he should always hustle and get the most out of plays. Jose took these words to heart, and used them to greatly improve his performance for the rest of the season.

He was in the midst of this burst of renewed enthusiasm when he received a phone call in 1984 that would change his life.

It was his sister, Teresa, calling him to let him know that their mother Barbara didn't have long to live. She had been suffering from headaches, and had developed a deadly blood clot situated right over her brain. This came as a complete shock. Barbara Canseco's health had been deteriorating over time, but the idea that one of his parents might actually pass away shocked the young ballplayer and gripped him with a deep sense of fear, dread, and anguish.

Jose didn't want to lose his mother, but after visiting her in the hospital, he had to accept that she wouldn't be around much longer. Hospital staff had informed the family that Barbara was brain dead, and that the life support that was keeping her bodily processes running would have to be turned off.

Knowing that the end was near, Jose Canseco promised at his mother's deathbed that he would do everything he could to make her proud. He would set his goals high and become the absolute best baseball player—as well as *the best person*—that he could possibly be.

He began regularly working out, eating right, and doing everything he could to improve his technique on the baseball field. All of this led to his grand debut in the Big Leagues, when he began playing for the Oakland Athletics in 1985.

Jose went on to have a stellar season in 1986, with a high RBI. But it was in 1987 when he really began to gain attention. This was partially thanks to his new teammate, Mark McGwire. These two power hitters made for a remarkable team, and were later named the "Bash Brothers" for how hard they could bash a baseball across the field.

Mark McGwire and Jose Canseco developed a healthy competitive relationship. Even while encouraging each other, they also tried to outdo each other on the baseball field. Jose was batting .257 at the time, and had 113 RBI. Jose and Mark also hit a combined total of 80 home runs that season.

These stunning combined home run stats had folks comparing the Bash Brothers with other dynamic pairings from the past, such as Willie Mays and Willie McCovey, or Mickey Mantle and Roger Maris. At the time, Maris held the record for the most home runs in a single season, with 61—but both Jose Canseco and Mark McGwire aimed to surpass that record.

Ultimately, it was Mark McGwire who did so. Meanwhile, Jose Canseco's career took a different track. In many ways, Jose peaked much sooner than Mark. Although Mark McGwire made history as the home run king in 1998, 10 years before that, in 1988, it was Jose Canseco who set a record by reaching the goal he had set for himself. He had publically declared to the press that he would become the "40 40 man" that year.

Jose believed that it was entirely possible for him to hit 40 homers and steal 40 bases during the 1988 season—and he was determined to do it. This was an interesting goal, since Eric Davis of the Cincinnati Reds had tried this very feat and failed during the previous season. The reason why achieving this objective is difficult in baseball is because it combines two rare and often mutually exclusive talents—agility and strength.

The most agile players are great base stealers, while the strongest players are typically the best equipped to hit home runs. That's not to say that no player is just as quick and agile as they are strong, but to be highly skilled in both areas is indeed a rarity. But Jose was one of those rare athletes, and he was determined to become the first "40 40 man."

Jose was viewed primarily as a big power hitter, but he was also fast. He had been a good runner for as long as he could remember, and knew that speed and agility were no problem for him. He knew what he could do, and he had publically set his goal. Now it was just a matter of making it happen.

By the fall of 1988, Jose was closing in on his record-breaking goal. He already had 39 home runs when the Oakland A's played against the formidable Kansas City Royals on September 18. The Royals had a tough-as-nails pitcher named Bret Saberhagen. Many wondered if Jose could handle Bret's powerful pitches, but sure enough, he was able hit his 40th home run during the game.

He now just had to steal his 40th base. This achievement proved to be a bit more elusive. As the season began to wind down, Jose had 38 stolen bases to his name. He needed to steal two more, and the window to do so was rapidly closing. But on September 23, he stole number 39 while playing against the Milwaukee Brewers.

This was a tough one, since Brewers pitcher Juan Nieves was quite good at shutting down base stealers. But Jose was a quick study, and watched Nieves very closely. He soon came to understand the pitcher's routine. After reaching first base, he found just the right moment to make his move, and ran for second. The pitcher threw the ball to second, but Jose Canseco was too fast. He was already there, having stolen his 39th base.

At this point, if anyone still doubted that he would reach 40, Jose Canseco was certainly not one of them. By the fifth inning of the same game, he was once again in position to steal another base. Interestingly enough, his fellow Bash Brother Mark McGwire was the one at bat. Canseco bided his time during the first pitch. But just as Juan Nieves wound up his second pitch and let it go, Jose Canseco ran like his life depended on it. Once again, he touched the base before the baseman could tag him out.

Jose was a happy man—or, more specifically, he was a happy *40 40 man*. This was a huge personal achievement for him, and the following year, things got even better. During the 1989 season, the Oakland Athletics won the World Series in a major sweep against the San Francisco Giants.

Jose Canseco faced a lot of challenges later on in life—including Congressional inquiries into steroid use—but even so, no one would ever forget what he had accomplished. History will always remember the incredible season when the Bash Brothers dominated, and Jose's record-setting 40 40 run.

FIVE FUN FACTS

- Jose was born in Cuba.
- He retired in 2003.
- Jose loves sports cars.
- He is accomplished in martial arts.
- He has a twin brother named Ozzie.

SOME TRIVIA!

Is it true that Jose Canseco once hit a home run with his head?

Yes! In one of the most infamous moments in baseball history, Jose Canseco was in the outfield trying to catch a ball hit by the opposing team, but instead it bounced off his head and went over the wall, technically making it a home run for the other side!

What special contest did Jose Canseco win during the 1986 season?

The MLB Home Run Derby.

Is it true that his mother went to a psychic who predicted Jose Canseco's future success?

Jose Canseco's dad—Jose Sr.—did an interview for Sports Illustrated in 1986, in which he claimed that Jose's mother had gone to a psychic prior to Jose's success in the MLB. It's claimed that this psychic told Jose's mother that one of her twin sons would become a smashing success in baseball.

What reality TV shows did Jose Canseco appear on?

The Surreal Life and Celebrity Apprentice.

Is it true that, during his time in the Minor Leagues, he once had to serve as batboy?

Yes, Jose Canseco claims that management and veteran players once made him serve as a batboy.

REAL-LIFE LESSONS

- Believe in yourself.
- Listen to your parents, coaches, and mentors.
- Take things in stride.
- Push yourself to do more.
- Set your goals, and then reach them.

TONY GWYNN KNOWS HOW TO WIN

Tony Gwynn was born in Los Angeles, California, on May 9, 1960, to Vendella and Charles Gwynn. Tony was nine years old when his mom and dad moved the family to Long Beach. They felt that this location had more to offer their kids in terms of schools and after-school programs, such as sports teams.

Tony's older brother, Charles Jr., played college baseball, and his younger brother, Chris, played on an MLB team later in life. His mom and dad, in the meantime, were both active in the community and supportive of their sons.

His dad was a hard worker who labored at a warehouse from 7:30 AM until 5:00 PM each day. But he also made time to coach his sons' Little League baseball team. His mother also worked long hours at the local post office, but she made sure to come out to support her son.

Tony's dad was not just a fan, but also a student of baseball. He knew everything about the history of the sport and the celebrated baseball greats of the past, such as Ty Cobb, Babe Ruth, and Willie Mays. Along with talking about baseball to his sons, he also made sure they played it. Tony's father set up their own makeshift baseball diamond in their backyard, right there in Long Beach.

The only problem with this miniature baseball diamond was that whenever Tony hit a home run over the wall, he was actually knocking the ball over a long-suffering neighbor's fence! If anyone remembers the baseball film *The Sandlot*, in which the kids knocked a ball over a fence, only to face an angry barking dog, this was basically a perfect portrayal of Tony's childhood. When the boys couldn't retrieve their balls, they had to resort to clobbering rolled-up socks!

It's safe to say that Tony Gwynn grew up with a love for the game. He took this love with him to Long Beach Polytechnic High School. He recalls school life being a diverse smorgasbord of cultures and interests. Along with being fun, baseball was a great way to break down any perceived barriers between the different cultures and backgrounds of his peers. No matter who they were or where they were from, baseball was a great equalizer that could bring folks together.

During high school, Tony played ball for a team called the Jackrabbits. He was a good player, and he was also seen as having a good head on his shoulders. He was viewed as a responsible young man who could lead and teach others. In fact, during the summers he served as a coach for a softball team. Of course, this included a lot of grunt work, such as painting foul lines and collecting all of the trash that made its way onto the field during games.

Along with baseball, Tony was a star basketball player. He was so good at basketball that at one point he considered quitting baseball so he could solely focus on basketball. It was actually his mother who managed to talk him out of doing so. She convinced him that he might regret it one day, and that it would be best to keep one foot in each sport, just in case. (Tony likely thanked his mom later, when she proved to be right!) At her suggestion, he continued to play both baseball and basketball when he moved on to college.

Tony played for San Diego State, where he became an all-star in both sports. His baseball team was called the Aztecs, and won the championship while he played for San Diego State. During his time with the Aztecs, Tony was often tapped as the designated hitter (DH). In baseball, it's common practice to designate one player to hit for the team's pitcher. This is viewed as beneficial for a variety of reasons, but most importantly because it spares star pitchers from potential injury and allows them to focus all of their energy on pitching.

Although he was a baseball star, Tony was still playing basketball, as well. Interestingly, he later credited the action of dribbling a basketball with strengthening his wrists. He believes that this extra wrist strength translated into a faster, stronger batting arm on the baseball field.

His hard work in college paid off, and in 1981 he was drafted by the San Diego Padres. Of course, he wasn't in the Big Leagues just yet. He still had to spend some time in the Minors while he worked his way up. He started spring training in San Diego the following year, and recorded a great batting average of .375. Then, during the season, he was shuffled over to Triple-A Hawaii.

After proving his worth on the Triple-A team, he was bumped up to the Padres official roster in 1982. He did well, at one point hitting a memorable double against Sid Monge, who was the relief pitcher for the Philadelphia Phillies. But following his big debut, he was plagued with a series of injuries that saw him sitting out for the start of the 1983 season.

Despite this setback, he persevered and began to refine his approach to the game. He wondered what he was doing wrong that caused him to get injured so much, and later claimed that he found the answer by watching video of himself playing. He was able to rewind the tape and look at where he was underperforming, and then correct it.

In the 1984 season, Tony managed to rack up some great stats. His batting average was .351, he had 71 RBIs, and he logged 33 stolen bases. He later maxed out with a .394 batting average. This remains the highest batting average recorded since 1941, when classic slugger Ted Williams averaged .406. For Tony to have been hitting such a high batting average this early in his career really says something.

Tony went on to play for 20 incredible seasons, always crediting his habit of watching himself on tape with allowing him to refine and improve every move he made on the field.

FIVE FUN FACTS

- Tony Gwynn has more batting titles than anyone else over the last 100 years.
- He holds several records for the Padres, for hits, doubles, triples, runs, RBIs, stolen bases, and walks.
- Tony Gwynn holds the highest per-season batting average since Ted Williams in 1941!
- He became friends with Ted Willaims toward the end of Ted's life.
- Tony used money from his signing bonus to buy a 1981 Monte Carlo.

SOME TRIVIA!

What's "Tony Gwynn's Opening Day?"

The second game of the season became known as Tony's "Opening Day, because he loved it when fans were dedicated enough to show up for game two of the season. To pay them back, he made it a habit to try his best on that day—which eventually became known as "Tony Gwynn's Opening Day."

What other sport did Tony play in college?

Basketball.

How many seasons did Tony play Major League baseball?

He played 20 seasons.

How many Gold Gloves did Tony win?

During his career, Tony was awarded five Gold Gloves.

What musical instrument did Tony play in junior high school?

The trombone.

REAL-LIFE LESSONS

- Listen to your elders.
- Do your best with what you have.
- Find commonalities and use them to connect with others.
- Play with passion.
- Pay attention to details.

RAFAEL PALMEIRO'S POWER HITS

Rafael Palmeiro was born in Havana, Cuba, on September 24, 1964. Rafael immigrated to the US with his family when he was still a small child. His family arrived in the US in 1971, and Rafael spent his formative years in Miami, Florida. The transition wasn't easy. Rafael later recalled how he initially struggled to learn English, and how it made him feel like an outsider.

He was placed with teachers who spoke his native language of Spanish, but even so, the fact that he missed portions of conversations among his peers weighed heavily on him. He often felt isolated and depressed.

Rafael can still remember what it was like on the mornings he had to get up for school, and how much he dreaded it. When his poor mom attempted to get him up out of his bed, he tried to act like he was still asleep. But no matter how much he tried to pretend, she would eventually succeed in getting him up and out the door.

Things changed for the better when Rafael managed to master English. He could now understand what the kids were saying, whether they spoke English or Spanish. This was a tremendous relief for him, and he no longer felt like an outsider. From this point forward, he excelled in school, and it wasn't long before he began to learn the fine art of hitting baseballs.

He was good at the sport, and those around him considered him to be a perfectionist. Rafael was always trying to improve his approach to batting, along with everything else he did in life. He was a standout star at Miami Jackson High School, and upon his graduation in 1982, he was ready to take things to the next level.

A short time later, Rafael was drafted by the New York Mets, but he wasn't quite ready to make such a big commitment. He had received a full scholarship to play for Mississippi State University, and felt that college ball would be a better transition for him.

He continued to stand out in college, where he managed to win the Southeastern Conference triple crown in 1984. Now feeling he was ready to go pro, he accepted a draft by the Chicago Cubs the following year, in 1985. But before he could play in the Big Leagues, he had to work his way up through the Minors.

He played ball on a Minor League contract that earned him just $700 a month. It was a modest start, but Rafael was just happy to be playing. He played for a Class A Minor League team based out of Peoria, Illinois, and when he did well, he was bumped up to the Double-A Eastern League for the 1986 season. There, he really rose to the occasion, hitting 12 home runs and reaching a batting average of .306. Anything above .300 is considered excellent, so it was clear that Rafael Palmeiro was a promising new batter to watch out for.

With all of his success, it wasn't long before the Big Leagues came calling. In fact, he was placed on the Cubs' roster in the middle of the 1986 season. Although he was briefly sent back to the Minor league in 1987, he was soon brought back to the Chicago Cubs Big League roster for the remainder of the season. After that, he spent the rest of his career in the Majors.

Changes came in 1988, when he was traded to the Texas Rangers. Rafael had gotten married and was ready to start a new life, so he and his wife moved down to Texas, where he could start fresh with his new team for the 1989 season.

That first year with the Rangers was rather lackluster for Rafael, as he only hit eight home runs. But this was likely just a matter of adjustment on his part, because he began to improve shortly thereafter. By the 1991 season, he was a batting leader, with 26 homers and a batting average of .322. These impressive stats led to Rafael being named most valuable player.

Rafael continued to rack up high marks in Texas, with his final season as a Ranger (1993) being one of his best. He then signed with the Baltimore Orioles, who gave him a large contract, which, including bonuses, amounted to $30 million. The move was bittersweet, as Rafael and his family had grown quite used to life in Texas. Nevertheless, Rafael was ready to start the 1994 season fresh, and he hit the ground running.

Before the season was over, he had managed to hit 23 home runs and reach a respectable, .319 batting average. By 1995, Rafael was regularly hitting over 30 home runs per season, and that particular year he had launched a total of 39 homers out of the park. He repeated the feat of hitting 39 homers in the 1996 season, helping the Orioles make it to the playoffs.

Despite the playoff berth, the team faced some surprising challenges, the most infamous of which occurred in a game against the New York Yankees. Derek Jeter, then a rising star on the team, had just hit a high, fly ball that should have been easily caught. Orioles outfielder Tony Tarasco just about had it in his glove, but as he reached up to grab the ball out of the air, fate—or, in this case, a 12-year-old boy—intervened. It was Yankees fan Jeffrey Maier, who reached out his glove and managed to make contact with the ball. He didn't catch it, but he did deflect it and cause it to change trajectory as it shot into the stands. The hit was deemed a home run, and Jeter was soon clearing all the bases for the New York Yankees.

Once they realized what had happened, and the Baltimore Orioles cried foul. Typically, fan interference disqualifies such a play—but the umpire refused to change his initial call. This infuriated the Orioles, but they had no choice but to let it go. Rafael knew that there was not point in arguing about it, and decided to simply make the best of a bad situation.

He and his teammates rallied, making a series of great plays, but it wasn't enough to beat the Yankees. The Yanks went on to the World Series, where they beat the Atlanta Braves.

After that fateful season, Rafael played a couple more years for the Orioles before returning to the Texas Rangers. He played for the Rangers from 1999 to 2003, then made a brief return to Baltimore for his last season before retirement.

In the meantime, Rafael had become something of a community leader—no matter where that community happened to be. Whether he was in Texas or Baltimore, Maryland, he found ways to give back. One of his pet projects was to deliver free baseball tickets to kids in need. The kids who got these tickets could take their families to watch baseball games, and were affectionately known as "Raffy's Rascals." It might not seem like much, but in both baseball and life in general, its often the little things that count the most.

FIVE FUN FACTS

- Rafael was the first player in the history of the Orioles to hit over 30 home runs three seasons in a row.
- He is a left-handed batter.
- Rafael has a half-brother named Jose Jr.
- He's an avid horse rider.
- He graduated from Miami Jackson High School.

SOME TRIVIA!

Is it true that Rafael dipped his hat in mud after a bad game?

Yes, he was known to do this all the way back in his days in the Minor League.

Does he have a nickname?

Yes, his teammates often called him "Raffy."

When did Rafael's family flee Cuba?

They left in 1971.

When did Rafael become a US citizen?

He became a citizen in 1988.

What high school did he go to?

Miami Jackson High School.

REAL-LIFE LESSONS

- Don't get discouraged when things get difficult.
- Take things as they come.
- Don't waste your time with non-productive arguments.
- Make the best of any situation.
- Do what you can to make a difference.

RICKEY HENDERSON
BATTER'S UP

Rickey Henderson made a name for himself due to his tremendous capacity to steal bases. But along with this unique skillset, he was also an incredible batter.

Rickey was born on Christmas Day—December 25, 1958. According to him, he was the Christmas gift that just couldn't wait. His mom and dad were in the process of making their way to the hospital when little Rickey made his debut ahead of schedule in the backseat of his parents' Oldsmobile.

Rickey's upbringing wasn't an easy one. His dad left when he was just two years old, and he bounced around a bit with other members of his family until his mother married a man named Paul Henderson. Rickey and his newly formed family unit then set down roots in Oakland, California. There, he grew up and learned to play ball, becoming a star player for Oakland Technical High School.

Along with baseball, he was also a great football and basketball player. It was actually football that won him a college scholarship. With dreams of playing for the Oakland Raiders in the NFL, he came close to accepting. It was only at the insistence of his mother that he ended up focusing his efforts on baseball instead. His mom advised him that a career in professional football had a much briefer shelf life than a career in baseball. Part of the reason she feared his football career might be short was due to Rickey's small size. She was afraid that her son would get injured and dropped from the team. Ultimately, she felt that her son was better built for baseball, and she wasn't afraid to tell him that.

Rickey listened to her, and ended up getting drafted by the Oakland Athletics in 1976, marking the start of his stint in professional baseball. His first Minor League team was the Boise A's. This was followed by time with the Modesto A's, which was where Rickey first became known for his ability to steal bases.

During the 1978 season, he was placed with the Jersey City A's, which was then part of the Eastern League. This was followed by a stint with the Navojoa Mayos during the 1978/1979 winter season, as part of the Mexican Pacific League. (Some players end up on Minor League teams in Canada, and others play for Minor League teams based out of Mexico!) Rickey led the Navojoa Mayos to victory in the Mexican Pacific League championship that season.

After this success, Rickey Henderson was called up to the Big Leagues in the summer of 1979, when he was placed on the official roster of the Oakland A's. The following year, he again made major waves by becoming only the third player in MLB history to steal 100 bases in one season.

This put him in some prestigious company, but Rickey Henderson was determined to aim even higher. At the same time, he had also become quite proficient with a baseball bat. His batting stance was something of an enigma for those who had to pitch to him. He had developed a very unique batting stance in which he crouched low to the plate, in order to make his strike zone much smaller. He also found that if he crouched low to the ground, he could see the ball coming much easier and compensate accordingly. It also increased his range and reach.

By the 1982 season, Rickey had perfected this batting stance so thoroughly that many pitchers didn't even want to deal with him. There were occasions in which they purposefully threw balls, just to walk Rickey to base and out of their sight.

Rickey's 1984 season saw him become more of a power hitter, hitting 16 home runs. The following year, he was traded to the New York Yankees, but he returned to the Oakland Athletics in the middle of the 1989 season. He did such a good job that year that he was named MVP. The Oakland Athletics also managed to make their way to the World Series that season, where they faced off against the neighboring San Francisco Giants.

These two California Bay Area teams were ready to go at it. The excitement was so great that you could almost feel the anticipation in the air. Perhaps it could be felt in the ground, too, because on October 17, 1989, when the entire Bay Area was rocked by a massive earthquake.

California is no stranger to quakes, but this one was bad and it did a lot of damage. The game was called off, and some people wondered if the entire World Series would be cancelled. However, proving the resiliency of baseball players and fans alike, the all-clear was given 10 days later to play ball once again. After all of the drama, the Oakland A's came out on top as the big winners of the World Series—or, as fans remember it, the "Earthquake Series."

Rickey Henderson was remembered for the tremors he made on the field during that series. In game three, he earned a double, a walk, and two steals. The next game, he treated fans to a home run. His overall batting average throughout the World Series remained high, but the standout feature of Rickey Henderson's performance as a batter was actually his eyes.

Rickey was highly adept at gauging whether or not he was being thrown a ball or a strike. All batters have this ability, to some extent, but Rickey seemed better than most. There were times when he simply refused to be struck out. He knew when to pull his swings and let the pitcher walk him to base. Rickey was the king of walks, leading the league in 1982, 1983, 1989, and 1998.

Rickey had a few more great seasons with the Oakland A's before being traded to the Toronto Blue Jays for the 1993 season. This was just a brief interlude, however, as he was back with the Oakland A's in 1994. By this point, along with a great batting average and the ability to steal bases, he had become known for having the gift of gab.

Rickey was a showman on the field, and often hammed it up with fans. He was known to carry on entire conversations with folks in the stands while he manned the outfield. Some thought that his antics were overdone, but Rickey shrugged any criticism off. He always insisted that sports existed to entertain people, and so that's what he did. Some thought he was arrogant or self-centered for "showing off," but Rickey always maintained that he was just trying to entertain the fans. To him, the people who wished he would tone it down were the selfish ones, since they cared more about their own image than they did the fans.

At the end of the day, Rickey saw baseball as a form of entertainment, and he understood him and his teammates to entertainers. He stuck to this philosophy all the way until his retirement. If it weren't for the fans, he wouldn't be paid to be a ballplayer, so he made sure that keeping them entertained and engaged was his number one priority.

FIVE FUN FACTS

- Rickey Henderson can bat with either hand.
- He's considered one of the best leadoff hitters in MLB history.
- He bats right-handed, but throws with his left.
- He has a record for most unintentional walks.
- Rickey Henderson retired in 2003.

SOME TRIVIA!

Does he have a nickname?

Yes! He was called the Man of Steal!

Who was Rickey's favorite MLB manager?

His favorite manager was Billy Martin. Billy's aggressive management style was unique, and ended up being called "Billy Ball."

How many different MLB teams did Rickey play for?

He played for nine different teams over the course of his MLB career.

How many bases did Rickey Henderson steal in the 1980s?

Rickey stole a whopping 838 bases in the 1980s!

What recording artist is Rickey named after?

He's named after Ricky Nelson.

REAL-LIFE LESSONS

- Listen to your parents, mentors, and other elders.
- Don't be afraid to be different.
- Make the best of the situations you are given.
- Be a leader, not a follower.
- Don't forget what's important (in Rickey's case, his fanbase).

I have included these free downloadable gifts to help light up your inner inspiration & reach your potential.

While you are reading through the stories, lessons and trivia, we recommend that you make use of all the bonuses we've attached here!

All our bonuses have been made specifically to help young athletes feel fired up, get inspired from the best to ever do it, and most importantly fall more in love with this incredible game!

Here's a list of what you're getting:

1) 250 Fun Facts From The World Of Sports
2) Sports Practice and Game Calendar
3) 5 Fun Exercise Drills for Kids
4) The BEST Advice From The Greatest Athletes Of All Time
5) The Mental Mindset Guided Meditation & Affirmation Collection
6) The Most Famous Events In Sports History And What They Can Teach Us

Now, it's over to you to scan the QR code, follow the instructions & get started!

IT'S NO BIGGIE
WITH CRAIG BIGGIO

If anyone ever burst onto the scene ready to swing, it was Craig Biggio. He was a star on his high school team, and once he graduated from Kings Park High School in New York, the MLB wasn't far behind.

But Craig was eager to prove himself in the college setting first, and in 1986 he took part in a collegiate summer baseball program with the Cape Cod Baseball League. He was an all-star stand out from the beginning, with an impressive batting arm, and performed alongside other future MLB greats such as Mo Vaughn and John Valentin.

Craig was drafted in the first round of the 1987 draft by the Houston Astros. Upon his arrival into the Big Leagues, he was first positioned as a catcher for the 1988 season. He loved being a catcher, but he also very much enjoyed stepping up to the plate to bat. During the course of his first season, he managed to log a relatively high .344 batting average.

A few years later, when the 1991 season rolled around, the introduction of fellow slugger Jeff Bagwell to the team sent Craig into overdrive. Jeff was a power hitter, just like Craig, and when he joined the Astros, the two formed their own dynamic duo, reminiscent of the Bash Brothers Mark McGwire and Jose Canseco. This powerful pairing became known as the "Killer B's" in light of the fact that they both had last names that began with a B. Jeff Bagwell ended up spending 15 seasons with Houston, and became a clear home run leader. But what about that other Killer B—Craig Biggio?

Craig eventually became recognized as a steady and predictable batter, with tremendous strength. But he was also kind of dirty! It became Craig's habit and trademark feature to not clean his batting helmet. The helmet was filthy, covered with grime and dirt, yet Craig thought the filth brought him good luck and refused to clean it.

Big changes came for Craig in the 1997 season, when the Astros hired a new manager by the name of Larry Dierker. Dierker could see Craig's potential and was interested in putting him in the lineup as a leadoff hitter. This wasn't always the safest of positions, however, and that year Craig was hit in the face by a baseball thrown by pitcher Geremi Gonzalez, in a game against the Chicago Cubs. Craig later described it as being similar to getting struck in the face with a "hammer."

Craig realized that he had a tendency to make himself a target, due to the fact that he had a habit of standing dead center in the middle of the plate. Other batters positioned themselves to the side of home plate, but not Craig—he liked to stand right on top of it. This gave him greater reach to hit balls that were just barely within the strike zone. But it also made him more likely to get hit by pitches. A lot of folks had a lot of fun with this. Kurt Snibbe of ESPN once even made a playable game for ESPN's official website called "Bean Biggio."

All jokes aside, it was this unique batting stance that allowed Craig to make some extraordinary hits. His stance was actually quite frustrating for pitchers, since it forced them to change their approach whenever he was at bat.

This unique batting stance led Craig and the Astros to the World Series in 2005. They ultimately lost to the Chicago White Sox, but both Craig and Jeff Bagwell enjoyed the ride.

Craig Biggio went on to make some major waves in the 2007 season, becoming the only Astros batter to ever reach 3,000 hits. However, the 2007 season also proved to be his last, as he retired at the end of the year.

Craig was a powerful and highly unusual batter who made his own style work for him. This is a great lesson for all of us. There isn't only one way to do things in life. If we are inventive enough, we might just find our own uniquely effective approach.

FIVE FUN FACTS

- Craig Biggio broke the hit-by-pitch record, due to being repeatedly hit by pitchers.
- Craig purposefully kept his batting helmet dirty.
- He was a talented football player in high school.
- In 2007, he joined the "3,000-hit" club.
- He played for the Houston Astros his entire MLB career.

SOME TRIVIA!

What was Craig Biggio's jersey number?

Number 7.

What's his full name?

Craig Alan Biggio.

Is Craig Biggio left-handed?

Technically, yes, since he writes with his left hand. But, oddly enough, he bats and throws with his right hand.

How many MLB teams did Craig Biggio play for?

Just one—the Houston Astros.

What year was Craig Biggio inducted into the Hall of Fame?

He was inducted in 2015.

REAL-LIFE LESSONS

- Work hard.
- Practice makes perfect.
- Be bold.
- Don't be afraid to take risks.
- Get back up when you fall.

ALEX RODRIGUEZ
YOU CAN'T ALWAYS BAT
A THOUSAND

In the early 2000s and 2010s, Alex Rodriguez (also known as A-Rod) absolutely dominated the league. But his ability didn't just form out of nowhere—it was developed. Alex owes a lot of his success to a mentor he had early on—Eddie Rodriguez. (Although Eddie carries the same last name as Alex, they are not related.) He was a volunteer coach at the local Boys Club who took Alex under his wing and began to teach him the game. Eddie definitely knew his stuff. In fact, he had served as a mentor and role model for several youngsters who later became professional baseball players.

Eddie convinced Alex that if he put in the effort, he could succeed. Eddie even bought Alex baseball gloves and other equipment, as if he were his own child. This proved incredibly useful when summer came around and Alex participated in baseball tournaments.

Alex continued to refine his talent, and by the time he was 14 he had decided that he was going to make a career out of baseball. He signed up for classes at a private high school called Westminster Christian, which was a special school in the Miami area known to have a great sports program. The school wasn't cheap, but Alex had good grades and qualified to have his tuition paid by way of a scholarship.

Alex was a dedicated student, and left home early in the morning to get to school. Due to his after-school activities, he typically didn't get back home until late in the evening, sometimes as late as 8:00 PM. He stayed busy, and his preoccupation with sports and academics kept him out of trouble.

By his sophomore year of high school, he was playing on three different sports teams for the school. He played shortstop for baseball, was the starting quarterback for football, and served as a point guard for the basketball team. Alex was determined to do well in all of these sports, but it was his performance on the baseball diamond that stood out the most.

His baseball coach, Rich Hofman, recognized Alex's potential early on. He could see that the kid had raw talent. By the time Alex was 16 years old, he was already an impressive batter. Even so, the coach knew that this raw talent needed a certain amount of refinement. Although Alex was a good hitter, his batting average was low—or at least lower than Coach Hofman thought it should be.

Coach Hofman realized that the reason Alex wasn't hitting more pitches was because he was too eager to hit. He was swinging at balls that he should have just let go. Coach Hofman made it his mission to teach Alex better discernment in the batting box, instilling in him the kind of judgment it takes to know a good pitch from a bad one.

Alex heeded this advice and began to watch much closer as the ball left the pitcher's hand. Soon, he was able to tell the difference between a good pitch and a bad one. He began picking and choosing which balls to swing at, and his batting average improved.

Alex's junior year proved to be a great one. His team took part in the World Junior Championship, which took them all the way to

Monterrey, Mexico. Alex was a leader during the Monterey games, hitting six home runs. He almost seemed destined to become a Major League player, but he didn't put all of his eggs in one basket. He was determined to make good grades, and planned to go to college.

Even though he was getting plenty of calls from scouts, he decided that the Big Leagues could wait in order for him to get a college education and play college baseball. Interestingly, this is the opposite approach that another young baseball slugger took that year, as Derek Jeter was drafted straight out of high school. The two players were around the same age, and by way of a mutual friend and a series of coincidences, they actually managed to meet each other during this crucial period.

Although Derek had been drafted by the New York Yankees, he was still making his way through the Minors at the time. He happened to be training with one of the Yankees Minor League farm teams based out of Florida, which brought him into close proximity with Alex. Thanks to their mutual friend, the two managed to meet and hang out.

During this initial meeting, Jeter served as a kind of mentor, explaining to Alex what he might deal with if he signed with an MLB team. He also explained the rigors of working one's way up through the Minor League farm system.

The meeting may have influenced Alex, as he had a change of heart. Although the University of Miami was ready to hand him a baseball scholarship, he decided to turn his attention to the MLB.

Alex ended up being selected first in the overall draft, by the Seattle Mariners. His deal was good—in fact, it was better than good. He was offered a three-year contract for $1.3 million, along with an additional $1 million signing bonus.

During the 1994 season, Alex began playing as a professional—albeit in the Minor League. He started out playing for the Appleton Foxes, which was a Class A farm team. He did well over the course of several games, hitting 11 home runs, which was enough to bump him up to a Class AA team—the Jacksonville Suns.

A few weeks later, he played his first game of Major League baseball with the Seattle Mariners, on July 8, 1994. He and his team played against the Boston Red Sox in Boston's famed Fenway Park.

During the 1995 season, Alex briefly returned to the Minors, playing for the Seattle Mariners' Triple-A affiliate team, the Tacoma Rainiers.

After this brief stint with Tacoma, he was bumped back up to the Seattle Mariners, where he finished a rather noteworthy 1995 season. The Mariners stormed across the country and ended up tying with the California Angels, eventually besting them just in time to seize the American League West title. During this impressive run, A-Rod hit his first Major League home run.

Alex was still learning the ropes, and at this point was way behind veteran batters, such as Jay Buhner, who hit 40 homers for the Mariners that same season. But Alex was a new, young player, and a steep learning curve was to be expected.

Alex really came into his own during the 1996 season. That year, he hit 36 home runs and logged a batting average of .358—not bad for a 21-year-old rising star! In fact, he was the third youngest baseball player to hit that many home runs in the MLB.

The 1997 season didn't go so well for Alex. After putting in a lackluster performance, he demonstrated just how frustrated he was. He had just been struck out by a skilled pitcher for the Toronto Blue Jays named Roger Clemens, and was so angry that he shouted and used profanity as he returned to the dugout. This temper tantrum was caught on live television and witnessed by his old coach, Eddie Rodriguez. Eddie called Alex up and told him that he needed to control his temper. He told him that such brash outbursts were inappropriate in someone he had mentored, and that he expected better of him.

Alex learned a lesson he would never forget, and promised to do better. And the 1998 season was indeed an improvement. Alex improved his reliability as a batter and managed to hit more than 40 home runs. This wasn't an all-time record in the MLB—in fact, that very same year, Mark McGwire hit a stunning 70 home runs. But it was a personal record for Alex Rodriguez, and he was thrilled to have reached such an important milestone. He ended the season with a total of 42 home runs and a desire to do even better the next time around.

Alex became a student of the sport, using highlight reels as his textbook of choice. He began to pour over footage of both himself and other players at bat. He wanted to learn exactly what the best batting technique was.

Alex eventually switched teams from the Seattle Mariners to the Texas Rangers at the beginning of the 2001 season. The hardest part of this transition was when he ended up playing against his old team, the Mariners. When he stepped onto the field, the same fans who used to cheer him now showered him with boos.

Alex could have taken this personally, but he shrugged it off as just being part of the game. He knew that fans cheered for their home team and booed the visiting players. Instead of taking offense, he reminded himself of all the good times he'd had with the Mariners, and of how nice the fans had been to him during his run in Seattle.

Alex learned to take it all in stride, and his efforts to maintain a healthy focus on the game paid off. He ended the 2001 season with 50 home runs and 200 hits. And the 2002 season was even better, with 57 home runs.

As good as he was, after the 2003 season, the Rangers decided to trade Rodriguez to the New York Yankees. Alex began batting for the Yankees in 2004, and was thrilled to be on the same team as his old friend Derek Jeter. But the 2004 season found Alex in a bit of a batting slump.

There were a lot of theories as to why this was the case. Many believe that Alex simply felt a lot of pressure to perform once he joined the Yankees. Alex himself often said that he felt as if he were starting all over again when he stepped into Yankee Stadium. He felt like all of the eyes were on him, and he folded under the pressure.

Alex learned yet another valuable lesson, which can be applied to both baseball and life in general—don't get too stressed out about doing good, or it will cause you to perform poorly!

Some stress is good, and can motivate you to do well, but too much stress can be debilitating. Alex learned this the hard way during that 2004 season. He wanted to perform when he started with the Yankees, but psyched himself out so badly that he ended up underperforming. He wanted to hit a homer every time he stepped up to the plate, only to strike out.

Eventually, he was able to regain his footing. Alex realized that he didn't have to constantly wow the crowd—he didn't always need to bat a thousand. He just needed to do his best. Alex carried this healthy attitude with him all the way to the World Series, which his team won in 2009.

FIVE FUN FACTS

- Alex later had a career as a sports analyst.
- He loves golf.
- He was known as a "clutch" player who could always perform critical plays at just the right time.
- Alex hit a total of 696 home runs during his career.
- His legacy is marred by the fact that he later tested positive for steroid use.

SOME TRIVIA!

Who were Alex's three favorite MLB players?

He was a big fan of Keith Hernandez, Dale Murphy, and Cal Ripken Jr.

What Renaissance artist does Alex admire?

He admires the work of Leonardo DaVinci.

What famous singer did Alex Rodriguez date?

He dated Jennifer Lopez.

How old was Alex when he reached the 500 club?

Alex hit his 500th homer when he was just 32 years old. This was the youngest that anyone had ever reached this milestone.

Alex led the league in what unique category?

Grand slams! In 2013, he broke Lou Gehrig's record of 23 grand slams by hitting his 24th. He ended his career with a total of 25.

REAL-LIFE LESSONS

- Listen to good advice.
- Be a good example—others are watching.
- Be detail-oriented.
- Learn from your mistakes.
- You don't have to be perfect. Just do your best.

JOEY VOTTO
HOW TO BE A REAL MVP

Joey Votto began life in Toronto, Canada, where he grew up the son of a couple of restauranteurs and wine enthusiasts named Joseph and Wendy Votto. Born in 1983, when Super Mario Bros. were just starting to make their rounds, Joey Votto grew up with a love of both videogames and baseball.

Joey went to Richview Collegiate Institute, a prestigious high school, where he played basketball and baseball, and even did a stint on a hockey team. After graduation, Joey intended to go on to college, but the Cincinnati Reds intervened, picking him in the 2002 MLB draft.

He had to prove his worth in the Minor League farm system before he could advance to the Majors. His first Minor League team was the Dayton Dragons, which was a Class A Midwest League team. He was a standout star with the Dragons, hitting 14 homers and logging a .302 batting average.

He was soon bumped up to the Class A Advanced Carolina League, where he managed to hit five homers over the span of 20 games, already making the case that he was going to be a future heavy hitter. He continued to work his way up in the Minors until he finally made his debut in the Big Leagues with the Cincinnati Reds during the 2007 season.

His first time at bat certainly wasn't his best—he struck out! He was able to rebound, however, and soon hit his first Major League homer. He ended the 2007 season with a batting average of .321.

His 2008 season was even better, with Joey actually breaking the record for most RBIs for a rookie player.

Joey started 2009 with a six-game hitting streak that lasted from April 12 to April 18[mr5] [CB6] . In 2010, he took things up a level and was named MVP. He was the team's most valuable player—and he proved to be valuable in more ways than one.

He might have been great at swinging a baseball bat and stealing a base or two, but it was his skills as an ambassador for the team that really made this Joey valuable. Even though he is an introvert, this quiet, thoughtful man began to warm up to both the press and the fans.

He gave extremely informative answers to the media, which they loved. But it was the fans who really got the best out of Joey. They soon began to realize that he was the most approachable player on the team. If anyone wanted an autograph, he was sure to give them one!

Unlike some other players, Joey didn't avoid his fans. He especially went out of his way to greet fans with taxing physical conditions or who were suffering from debilitating illnesses. The time he gave to these fans grew into the Joey Votto Foundation in 2013. This charitable organization was created to help those who have been affected by post-traumatic stress disorder.

Joey's philanthropic efforts have been recognized by the league, and he was nominated in both 2021 and 2022 for the "Roberto Clemente Award," which is given to MLB players who has gone above and beyond to give back to their communities.

FIVE FUN FACTS

- Joey was born in Toronto.
- He has three younger brothers.
- He's a member of the Canadian Baseball Hall of Fame.
- Joey played for Team Canada in the World Baseball Classic.
- He has a passion for spreading awareness about mental health.

SOME TRIVIA!

What's his full name?

Joseph Daniel Votto.

How many times was he MVP?

Two times.

What board game does Joey like to play?

Chess.

How many Silver Slugger awards has Joey won?

Four.

When did Joey become a US citizen?

Joey Votto is a Canadian native, but became an official United States citizen in 2022.

REAL-LIFE LESSONS

- Don't be afraid to try.
- Learn from adversity.
- Be a team player.
- Give back to the community.
- Be kind.

FRANK THOMAS STEPS UP TO THE PLATE

Frank Thomas got his start in Columbus, Georgia, where he was born in 1968. In high school, he played both baseball and football, and his baseball team won a state championship. By Frank's senior year in 1986, he was eager to be drafted into the Big Leagues. But first he had to deal with a disappointing delay.

Part of the reason that baseball scouts passed Frank up was his sheer size. He was a big guy, even in high school, standing 6 foot 5 and weighing 240 pounds. They may have felt he was better suited for football than baseball. Frank didn't have much of a choice, so he fell back on his football skills and earned a scholarship from Auburn University.

Despite the fact that he had to focus on football, he still kept one foot in baseball, playing on both teams at the university. He played baseball for the Auburn Tigers, scoring a high batting average and becoming a favorite of Auburn baseball coach Hal Baird. He actually managed to set a record for home runs, hitting 49 homers.

Along with being able to hammer the ball, Frank showed great discernment that belied his young age. Unlike many young players who were eager to hit just about any ball thrown their way, Frank already had the ability to know when to swing and when to wait.

As soon as the ball left a pitcher's hand, he knew where it would go. If it was destined to curve too far to the right or left, he knew to let it fly on by so that it could be called a "ball." In the game of baseball, pitches that are thrown out of the strike zone are known as "balls." If the batter does not swing at them, they do not count against them. If the batter manages to get four balls, they are allowed to walk to first base.

During his time playing college baseball, Frank was walked 38 times over the course of 59 games, proving his ability to distinguish a good pitch from a bad one. In many other ways in life, he also showed a similar sense of discernment.

By his second year of college ball, Frank had a high batting average of .385. At this point, he was also spending summers playing for an amateur team called the Orleans Cardinals.

His final year playing college ball was in 1989. That season, Frank was named MVP, with 19 home runs and a batting average of .403. Although a high batting average in the MLB and a high batting average in college baseball are two different things, this was still very impressive—and good enough to finally gain the attention of Major League scouts.

On June 5, 1989, Frank's dream came true when the Chicago White Sox picked him in the first round of the draft.

He still had to work his way up through the Minors, but Frank was more than willing to take on the challenge. His first Minor League team was the Gulf Coast White Sox. During his time with this team, he managed to record a batting average of .365. This good showing resulted in an invite to attend the 1990 spring training with the official Chicago White Sox team.

The next thing Frank knew, he had made it into the Big Leagues. He first played as an official member of the White Sox on August 2, 1990. After a couple of months of playing, he had a batting average of .330. This was fantastic, since the MLB average at that time was .259.

He also maintained his discerning eye, and earned 44 walks. Skilled pitchers literally threw everything they had at Frank—curve balls, fast balls, screw balls, you name it. But he wasn't falling for it. He knew a good pitch when he saw it, and he refused to swing at anything that wasn't within the strike zone.

Frank's ability behind the bat helped the Chicago White Sox have a much better season in 1990 than they had in recent years. Fans noticed, as well, and there was excitement in the stands as the White Sox began to enjoy success.

In 1991, Frank was made the designated hitter, which put him in a position to truly show what he could do. As testament to both his hitting and walking ability, he made it to base at least once in 62 out of the 63 games that he played. He may not have always hit a home run, but whether through singles, doubles, triples, or just getting walked, he was almost always heading in the right direction.

Frank Thomas proved to be an interesting batter. His swings were not just powerful, but also inside out. Frank had what's known as an "inside-out swing," which means that when he swings, he let's go of his top hand from the bat first, rather than the bottom one.

This allows him to hit the ball much later than he would be able to otherwise. Many inside out batters benefit from this, since it gives them a longer window of time to figure out what to do with the ball. We're talking a split second difference here—but there are occasions in baseball when a split second can make all the difference in the world.

Frank hit 32 homers that season, and by the start of 1992 around, he was clearly a rising star. He even got the attention of Hollywood, which cast him in the film *Mr. Baseball*, alongside Tom Selleck. It was just a walk-on role, but for the guy who specialized in knowing when to walk, it couldn't have come at a better time.

During the 1993 season, Frank truly rose to the occasion, becoming a power hitter who launched 41 homers. This made him far and away the best slugger on the team. In fact, none of his fellow White Sox teammates hit more than 22 homers that year.

The 1994 season was an abbreviated one due to a strike, but Frank still managed to hit 38 home runs. And he kept it up over the next 10 years, eventually leading the White Sox to the World Series in 2005. The White Sox stunned the world and came out on top, winning a World Series for the first time in 88 years. Realizing that he was getting older and wanting to go out on top, Frank decided to move to another team after that championships.

He was looking for a change, and the Oakland Athletics provided it to him. He played with them for a season before switching to the Toronto Blue Jays. Then Frank went back to the A's for another year before failing to find a team in 2009.

Realizing he wanted to get back to where he had started, Frank signed a new contract with the Chicago White Sox as the 2010 season began. But he only signed a contract for one day! He did this so that he could play one more game with his original team, on February 12, 2010, before announcing his intention to retire from the MLB.

FIVE FUN FACTS

- In high school and college, Frank Thomas was as much a football star as he was a baseball star.
- Frank hit his 500th career home run on June 28, 2007.
- He loves to cook.
- His walk-up song when he played for the Chicago White Sox was the AC/DC tune "Back in Black."
- Frank won the "Silver Slugger Award" four times, in 1992, 1993, 1994, and 2000.

SOME TRIVIA!

Did he have a nickname?

Yes! They called him "The Big Hurt."

How many times was he the MVP?

Two times.

What was Frank's jersey number for the Chicago White Sox?

His jersey number for the White Sox was 35, and was officially retired in 2010.

How many times was he an All-Star?

Five times.

When was he inducted into the Hall of Fame?

He was inducted in 2014.

REAL-LIFE LESSONS

- Don't give up on your dreams.
- Frank was great at recognizing when curve balls were thrown his way. Likewise, use your own critical thinking to identify the potential curve balls in your life.
- Try a unique approach.
- Diversify your talents.
- Frank Thomas left the White Sox on a high note. Learn when to move on.

I have included these free downloadable gifts to help light up your inner inspiration & reach your potential.

While you are reading through the stories, lessons and trivia, we recommend that you make use of all the bonuses we've attached here!

All our bonuses have been made specifically to help young athletes feel fired up, get inspired from the best to ever do it, and most importantly fall more in love with this incredible game!

Here's a list of what you're getting:

1) 250 Fun Facts From The World Of Sports
2) Sports Practice and Game Calendar
3) 5 Fun Exercise Drills for Kids
4) The BEST Advice From The Greatest Athletes Of All Time
5) The Mental Mindset Guided Meditation & Affirmation Collection
6) The Most Famous Events In Sports History And What They Can Teach Us

Now, it's over to you to scan the QR code, follow the instructions & get started!

MANNY RAMIREZ
GOOD NEWS FROM
THE BATTER'S BOX

Manny Ramirez was born in 1972, in a country that has become almost synonymous with great baseball players—the Dominican Republic. Manny immigrated to the US when he was still a teenager. He settled with his family in a neighborhood in New York, and played baseball for his high school. He led his team to championships, and at one point was named Public Schools Athletic League High School Player of the Year.

Manny was on the fast track to success. Upon graduating from high school, he was drafted by the Cleveland Indians. He spent a relatively short amount of time in the Minors before he made his Major League debut on September 2, 1993.

His first game was a bit of a bust, but he came alive during his second game, when he managed to hit a couple of home runs and a double. His next season, however, was interrupted by the infamous 1994 baseball strike, so Manny didn't really have the chance to show the world what he could do with a baseball bat until 1995. That year, his batting average rose to .308. The Indians also made it to the World Series, but fell short of winning it.

The Indians once again made it to the World Series in 1997, but again failed to take home the trophy. From this point forward, Manny tried his best to improve his own personal game, whether his team made it to the final series or not. In 1999, he recorded

165 RBIs in one season. The last time anyone else in the league had cracked this mark was 1938.

Manny still had his heart set on winning a World Series, but he wouldn't do it with the Cleveland Indians. He was eventually traded to the Boston Red Sox, where he charged full steam ahead, all the way to the 2004 World Series.

This was a major event in Boston, since the Red Sox hadn't won the World Series since the "Curse of the Great Bambino" in 1918, when they traded home run slugger Babe Ruth (affectionately known as the Bambino).

Manny wasn't superstitious, and he believed that he and his teammates could win. As it turned out, he was right! With the iconic victory of the Boston Red Sox in 2004, he secured his first World Series win. Manny played a big part in all of this, and was even named World Series MVP.

The following year saw another personal milestone for Manny, when he managed to hit his 400th home run. Then, two years later, Manny and the Red Sox won another World Series in 2007, beating out the Rockies in seven games, 4-3.

Manny has since developed a reputation for having some rather unique interests. On one occasion, he converted his sunglasses into a personal MP3 player, allowing him to listen to music while he was out catching fly balls! He's also known to trick out his cars with all of the latest gadgets. For Manny, a car is not complete unless its decked out with eye-catching LED lights and full of computer and TV monitors.

Manny is also quite generous. He once auctioned off one of his customized cars and donated the proceeds toward a charity sponsored by the LA Dodgers. He is also part of another great charitable organization known as CHARLEE that helps poor and mistreated children.

Manny hit another milestone in 2008, when he hit his 500th home run. This put him in the rare 500 club, which only counts 28 other players as members. A short time later, he was traded to the Dodgers, with whom he played until 2010.

Whether he was hitting home runs, tricking out cars, or giving back to the community, Manny was always just being Manny. He stayed true to himself throughout his life and career, and his courtesy and kindness has always shone bright.

FIVE FUN FACTS

- Manny used to write words of encouragement (and sometimes chastisement of his opponents!) on the bottoms of his shoes before games.
- He dropped out of high school, but later got his GED.
- He loves tricked-out cars.
- He met his wife Juliana while working out in the gym. [mr7] [CB8]
- Manny once stuck a paycheck in one of his shoes, only to later forget that he put it there.

SOME TRIVIA!

Manny is a unique guy—so much so, that the explanation of his oddities became a unique catchphrase in itself. What was that catchphrase?

"It's just Manny being Manny!"

Is it true that Manny Ramirez is afraid of the dark?

According to former teammate Pedro Martinez, it's true. During an interview for *Sports Illustrated*, Pedro claimed that when they were on the road, Manny would barge into Pedro's hotel room to have a "sleepover" because he was afraid to be alone in the dark.

What Manny do 12 times?

He was a 12-time All-Star.

How many times did he win the Silver Slugger award?

Nine times.

What Sega Genesis game did he appear on?

World Series Baseball '96.

REAL-LIFE LESSONS

- Persevere.
- Believe in yourself.
- Practice makes perfect.
- Learn from your mistakes.
- Pay attention to details.

KIRBY PUCKETT LEARNING TO LIVE AND LET LIVE

The baseball phenomenon known as Kirby Puckett was born on March 14, 1960. Born and raised in Chicago, Kirby learned pretty quickly what the hard knocks of life were all about. His dad worked around the clock, holding two jobs—one at the post office and the other at a department store. He was gone most of the time, and it was up to Kirby's mother to raise him and his other siblings.

Kirby grew up in a low-budget apartment in the projects. Those who lived there did so out of necessity. In the projects, poverty, crime, and desperation a normal part of life.

Not only was life hard, but it could also be quite boring—so boring, in fact, that Kirby entertained himself by throwing a baseball against the wall. If you have ever lived in an apartment and heard a repeated thump on the other side of the wall, and wondered what it could be—maybe it is a future MLB hopeful like Kirby, practicing his throwing arm!

The biggest problem Kirby had was when he and his buddies played outside of the apartment complex, as they ran the risk of provoking the wrath of the maintenance man. Playing ball outside tended to mess up the grass, and the maintenance man didn't appreciate the muddy mess Kirby and his friends left behind.

Nevertheless, Kirby stayed busy perfecting his game. By the time he reached high school, he ranked as an All-American. After he graduated from high school in 1979, he hoped to be drafted by the MLB, but was disappointed when he didn't immediately get an invite.

Kirby ended up working on the assembly line at Ford, putting carpets in cars instead. Interestingly, even though he was working on the interior of cars every day, he didn't have a car himself. Kirby Puckett rode the bus to work. He couldn't help but wonder if there might be something better for him in life.

Kirby's baseball dreams were revived when he managed to snag a baseball scholarship from Bradley University. He played for the Bradley Braves, where he was known as quite a slugger. By the time the 1981 season came to a close, he had managed to hit eight home runs and secure a batting average of .378. He was also named Player of the Year for the National Junior College Athletic Association.

After college, Kirby played in the Minor League system before playing his first Major League game for the Minnesota Twins in 1984. During his first few seasons, he emerged as a great singles hitter. He then expanded his reach—big time.

By the time Kirby and the Twins reached the World Series in 1987, he was a power hitter. The Twins won the World Series that year, trouncing their opponents, the St. Louis Cardinals. This win—and the important role that Kirby played in it—made Kirby Puckett a household name. He learned the hard way, however, how fame can have its fair share of challenges.

The first taste of the downside of fame was during one of the subsequent victory parades in downtown Minneapolis, Minnesota. Kirby's car was mobbed by fans, and for some odd reason, they thought it was a good idea to hurl toilet paper rolls at the motorcade. After getting pelted with a few rolls of double soft, Kirby had had enough.

Even worse was when fans recognized him in public places and demanded autographs at the most inopportune of times. He was out shopping with his family on one occasion when a lady approached and asked him to give autographs to her children. Kirby had his hands full, and wasn't able to do so at the time. He tried to explain as much to the lady, but she became so irate she started shouting and using profanity. Finally, after she realized that she wasn't going to get her way, she made her exit, still berating Kirby on her way out.

It's incredible that a "fan" could turn on their hero so quickly, but Kirby learned to take such things in stride. He realized that fame, and even just being around famous people, can cause folks to do some rather bizarre things. That didn't excuse their behavior, but his understanding of this better prepared him to deal with such things in the future.

Kirby kept his head up and kept working hard. He led his team to another World Series victory in 1991. In fact, it was Kirby Puckett who hit the game-winning homer in the pivotal sixth game. This allowed the Twins to move forward to game seven, which they won to clinch the World Series championship.

The next two seasons were not quite as exciting for the team. Kirby did well in the 1992 and 1993 seasons, and ended the 1993 season by performing in the All-Star Game, where he was named MVP. But his team as a whole lagged behind.

The 1994 season was cut short by a strike, but it was in the 1995 season when Kirby faced the biggest challenge of his career. This was the year when he took a fast ball to the face from pitcher Dennis Martinez.

Players get hit in baseball all the time, but this hit was particularly bad, and Kirby ended up with a shattered jaw. Fans were shocked to see Kirby fall over with blood pouring from his head. Martinez felt horrible about the incident and profusely apologized to Kirby (and anyone else who would listen). Fortunately for him, Kirby had a forgiving nature and accepted the apology. Despite the terrible pain he suffered, he considered it an innocent mistake. As soon as he was healed up enough to talk, he went on the record to state, "I know he didn't mean to hit me. Dennis is a good friend of mine, and I know it wasn't intentional."

After his injury, Kirby first returned to the batter's box on March 27, 1996. It was challenging to stand there and face that pitcher's mound once again, but Kirby was able to get right back into the swing of things. He hit the ball an estimated 450 feet, right down the center of the field. He then hit a similar far ball into left field.

It seemed like Kirby was back. Unfortunately, the next morning, he woke up to find that his vision was oddly impaired in his right eye. Considering what had happened to him when he was hit by that fast ball, it was natural to think that the injury had something to do with it, but it was discovered that Kirby suffered from a seemingly unrelated yet devastating condition. He was diagnosed with glaucoma, which is a disease of the eye that can lead to blindness.

At first, it was believed that much of the damage could be reversed with treatment, but soon it was realized that this was not the case. Knowing that his baseball career was over, Kirby announced his retirement. The 1996 season was his last, and at just 36 years old, he hung up his bat for good. Sadly, Kirby only lived 10 more years, passing away from a massive hemorrhagic stroke on March 5, 2006.

FIVE FUN FACTS

- During Game 6 of the 1991 World Series, he halfway climbed a wall and made a crucial game-deciding catch.
- Kirby retired in 1996.
- In 2001, he was inducted into the Hall of Fame.
- He established the Kirby Puckett Youth Foundation to help give back to the community.
- Kirby was known as the "Twins Ambassador."

SOME TRIVIA!

How many teams did Kirby play for?

Just one—the Minnesota Twins.

What's his favorite food?

Anything grilled! He loved cookouts.

How many World Series did he win?

Two.

How old was Kirby when he retired?

He was 36 years old.

What was his favorite hobby?

He loved to fish.

REAL-LIFE LESSONS

- Do the best with what you have. All Kirby had was a wall and a ball!
- Find your strength through adversity.
- Be gracious.
- Forgive others. If Kirby could forgive the pitcher who hit him in the face, we can do the same.
- Be grateful.

SAMMY SOSA
ALWAYS DO YOUR BEST

Sammy Sosa was born on November 12, 1968, in the Dominican Republic. Shortly after he learned to walk, Sammy first picked up a baseball. Baseball has been an incredibly popular sport in the Dominican Republic ever since it was first introduced in the 19th century, so it was almost inevitable that Sammy would be drawn to the sport.

Sammy grew up poor. His father passed away when he was just seven years old, and ever since then Sammy did what he could to make money for his family. He first did so through shining shoes, which was a common practice in the Dominican Republic. He used a rag and a bit of shoe polish to clean up the footwear of strangers in exchange for a little bit of cash. It was grueling and humbling work, but little Sammy did it all with a smile. He learned from a young age that life is what you make it. No matter the circumstances, you can make the best of it. Sammy didn't let his poverty or the grueling nature of his work bring him down.

He also found time to play baseball—or at least his version of it. When he wasn't in school or trying to earn a little extra money on the side, Sammy could be found in a back alley or an open field, playing ball with his buddies. Since they were usually lacking equipment, they had to use a stick for a bat and a rolled-up sock for a ball. But whatever they lacked in gear, they made up for with enthusiasm.

One particular variation Sosa enjoyed was a game in which he and his friends hit the cap of a water bottle with a stick. The pitcher in this little game actually threw the bottlecap like a frisbee, allowing it to spin through the air, while the batter tried their best to whack it with the stick. The fact that the batter had to hit an object much smaller than a baseball required exemplary skills. You have to have good eyes to whack a bottlecap!

That keen eyesight and aim Sammy developed as a child aided his career as a baseball player. When Sammy was 14 years old, he began to play on an official baseball team. He perfected his skills and, in 1985, gained the attention of a scout named Kiki Acevedo.

Kiki liked what he saw, and had Sammy come to a local baseball tryout. He was ultimately signed by the Texas Rangers on July 30, 1985. Sammy was only 16 years old when he became a professional ballplayer. He bounced around in the Minors for a few years before the Majors came calling.

Sammy's big break into the Big Leagues came in 1989, when he debuted with the Texas Rangers. His first game with the Rangers took place on June 16, 1989, when he and his team faced off against the New York Yankees. He wasn't hitting homers right out the gate, but he did have a couple solid hits during his first game in the Major Leagues. His first homer actually came a few days later, on June 21, when the Rangers played against the Boston Red Sox.

It typically takes some time for a rookie to find their groove in the Big Leagues, but the fact that Sammy was developing so quickly was a clear demonstration of his potential. He soon caught the eye of Larry Himes, who was GM for the Chicago White Sox. Mr. Himes was impressed with both his skill and determination, and decided to try and recruit Sammy for the White Sox. It worked, and Sammy was traded later that summer.

During the 1991 season with the White Sox, Sammy logged a .340 batting average and seemed poised to improve his fame even further. But his time with the White Sox was brief, ending after just one season. He then had his longest MLB stint with the Chicago Cubs, whom he played for from 1992 to 2004.

Sammy started out slow with the Cubs, and was hampered by injuries. But by 1993, his batting average had ticked up to a respectable .261 and he had hit 33 homers for the year. The 1994 season was even better, with Sammy earning the coveted "triple crown." This is achieved when a batter leads the league in batting average, home runs, and RBIs. He achieved a batting average of .300, hit 25 homers, and managed to reach 70 RBIs.

The 1994 season was a shortened one due to a baseball strike, so folks were left wondering just how good Sammy might have been if he hadn't been interrupted. But the 1995 season was Sammy's time to shine. He ended up hitting 36 home runs and stealing 34 bases. He also hit an impressive number of homers in 1996, one of the most infamous of which was launched so far out of Chicago's Wrigley Field that it smashed into a window in an apartment building across the way. The tenants were likely fairly upset, until they learned just how valuable that Sammy Sosa ball was! Years later, memorabilia of that type sold for a hefty price.

An injury put Sammy out for the second half of the 1996 season, and his slow recovery impacted the 1997 season, as well. He didn't quite get his footing again until the 1998 season, when he and Mark McGwire had their infamous "home run chase." Up until that point, the record for most home runs in a season was held by legendary batter Roger Maris back in 1961, when he hit 61 homers. Both Mark McGwire—who played for the St. Louis Cardinals at the time—and Sammy Sosa were determined to beat the record, and they developed a healthy competition along the way. Sosa, as humble as ever, even called his competitor Mark McGwire his hero and idol. Mark McGwire returned the love, and there were even times he could be seen playfully blowing kisses to Sammy Sosa from the field!

Although it might not always be recommended to blow kisses to your chief rival, this should serve as a great lesson to us all about how to behave in a good-natured manner, both on and off the field.

On September 7, 1998, the two faced off at Mark McGwire's home field in St. Louis. Mark had 60 home runs, while Sammy had 58. Mark quickly sealed the deal by hitting number 61, and Sammy was seen taking off his glove and breaking out in applause. But the chase was not yet over.

Sammy eventually reached 60, then 61, and even 62. In fact, both players were tied at 62 for some time. The chase continued, and for a brief moment, on September 16, Sammy was actually ahead of Mark McGwire with 66 homers (to McGwire's 65). But his lead didn't last long, as Mark also hit his 66th homer an hour later.

Mark McGwire went on to finish the season with what was then a record 70 home runs, while Sammy Sosa finished with 66. Sammy had several more great years ahead of him, but he never forgot that 1998 season and the lessons he learned, both on and off the field.

FIVE FUN FACTS

- Sammy's full name is Samuel Peralta Sosa.
- Sammy hit his 400th homer during his 1354th game.
- In 2005, he testified before Congress about accusations of steroid use. He denied those accusations.
- His nickname is "Mikey."
- He attended Bill Clinton's State of the Union Address as a special guest in 1999.

SOME TRIVIA!

Sammy Sosa is one of only nine players to have done what?

He hit over 600 homers during his career.

Was Sammy involved in music?

Yes, Sammy has worked with other artists, and has also made recordings of his own.

What special award did Sammy receive?

He received the "Roberto Clemente Award" for his efforts in giving back to the community.

How many times was he an All-Star?

Seven times.

When did he become a US citizen?

He became a US citizen in 1995.

REAL-LIFE LESSONS

- Be industrious.
- Maintain a positive attitude, regardless of your circumstances.
- Develop a regular practice routine.
- Be gracious to competitors—Sammy Sosa counted his rival Mark McGwire as a friend.
- Enjoy the game, and enjoy life!

PAUL MOLITOR
GOES TO BAT

Paul Molitor began his life on August 22, 1956, in St. Paul, Minnesota, where he was born to Richard and Kathy Molitor. He was one of eight kids in the family, and in many ways the big family he grew up in served as his first team. With his siblings, he learned what it was like to cooperate, work together, and solve any potential disputes. He had to learn the art of sharing and compromise. If someone wanted a toy, or merely extra time in the bathroom, negotiations inevitably had to be made.

Paul grew up loving baseball, and upon enrolling at Cretin High School in St. Paul, he became an active part of the school's baseball team, the Cretin Raiders. He was a star player, and by his senior year, he began to be approached by MLB scouts. Windows of opportunity were also opening for him to play college ball, as the University of Minnesota, the University of Arizona, and Creighton University were all prepared to offer him scholarships. Having always wanted to get a college education, Paul chose to go to school.

Paul enrolled at the University of Minnesota, where he played shortstop for the Minnesota Golden Gophers. He managed to earn All-American honors, then was drafted by the Milwaukee Brewers in the 1977 MLB draft. He played in the Minors for a year before making his Big League debut for the Milwaukee Brewers in 1978.

By the time the 1980 season rolled around, Paul had found his groove, logging a batting average of .358. He had developed good habits when it came to choosing between good pitches and bad ones. But, at the same time, Paul had developed a very bad habit.

During this period, Paul had become mixed up with cocaine. Cocaine is a dangerous, highly addictive drug that came into wide use among baseball players in the late 1970s and early 1980s. Like many of his peers, Paul began experimenting with the drug just for fun. He enjoyed the energetic and euphoric boost the drug initially gave him. But, as is the case with all drugs, that euphoria was fleeting, and he soon realized the drug was doing more harm than good.

Not wanting his baseball career to be consumed by drug use, Paul decided to quit cold turkey. If someone quits cold turkey, it means that they just stop and never try it again. Not everyone can do it—and many addicts end up returning to drugs later. Fortunately for Paul, his efforts were successful. However, he realized that others were not quite as successful in kicking the habit. This realization inspired him to do volunteer work in his downtime, as a spokesperson and counselor to help others who were battling drug addiction. He even showed up at schools to discuss the dangers of drugs with students.

Paul was happy to get a fresh start, but the 1982 season had its own unique set of challenges. It proved to be a rough one, not just for Paul, but for virtually all of the batters on the Milwaukee Brewers. That season, the MLB seemed to have a whole new crop of top-of-the-line pitchers, and it had suddenly become exceedingly challenging to rack up a lot of good hits.

To make matters worse, during this particularly challenging season, Paul was hit in the head with a baseball by pitcher Milt Wilcox. It's always scary when a batter gets struck like this, but, fortunately for Paul, the injury didn't seem to be a serious one. He was stunned and in pain, but nothing was broken, and he was able to get right back to bat immediately afterwards.

Paul and his team made something of a late comeback that season. They were victorious in a stunning match against the Baltimore Orioles, which helped them make their way to the 1982 World Series, where they faced off against the St. Louis Cardinals. This was an interesting matchup. The Brewers were known as heavy hitters, while the Cardinals employed a much more finessed strategy, with a greater emphasis on fast running and defense, rather than hitting homers.

Paul was in excellent form, and making great hits—one of which was even made off of a broken baseball bat. But the Brewers came up short in the World Series that year and were bested by the Cardinals.

The 1983 season found Paul in a bit of a slump. His batting average actually dropped down to an underwhelming (at least for him) .270. He also faced sickness and injury, which slowed him down. Paul just wasn't feeling the same, and neither was his team. They had begun to shed some of their old crew, and there was a great reshuffling in the works.

Paul was in his late 20s at the time, and hated to say goodbye to the guys he had established relationships with. But he was young and had his whole career ahead of him, and there were plenty more friends to make along the way—both on and off the field. Paul had gotten married to a woman named Linda, and in 1984 they started a family with the birth of their first child—a girl named Blaire.

The 1986 season opened with a lot of promise, and Paul came out of spring training camp ready for action. He ended up being the designated hitter that season, an important role for any batter. But he was once again sidelined by a spate of injuries. At one point, he tore his right hamstring chasing a ball, and that injury took him out of the game for several weeks. Even so, he managed to recuperate by the end of the season and make a comeback, earning several memorable hits for the team. In particular, a victory against the Cleveland Indians was remembered rather fondly after the Brewers won in a spectacular 5-3 finish.

The 1987 season saw the Brewers embark upon a 13-game winning streak, with Paul leading the charge. The first game of the season was a win for the Brewers, and by April 14, they already had seven wins under their belt. During the eighth game, Paul launched a homer right out the gate. He later recalled this being one of the first times that he had enjoyed playing baseball in a long time. He and his teammates were so happy just to play ball that they didn't worry about anything else. This happiness seemed to take the edge off, which was just what the team needed.

Paul learned a great lesson that year. The more you enjoy what you do, *the better you will do it*. Paul later spoke at length about the mental aspect of the game. He said that he learned that once you come out on top in your mind, the rest will typically follow. There's a battlefield being fought on the baseball diamond, but there's also one going on in your head. Paul learned how to conquer both during that spectacular 1987 season.

Paul's run with the Brewers was great while it lasted, but life is full of changes, and in 1993 he moved to the Toronto Blue Jays. The Blue Jays were really a perfect team for his unique style, because they used a consistently strategic, multifaceted approach.

They had strategic hitters like Paul, but also incredible baserunners such as Roberto Alomar and Rickey Henderson, who could not only run, but who were also gifted in the art of the steal.

Through a combination of well-placed hits and well-timed stolen bases, the Blue Jays presented a formidable challenge to whomever they played against.

While playing with the Blue Jays, Paul truly came into his own as a power hitter. He ran up a batting average of .332 that season, and launched 22 homers. He also led the Blue Jays to the World Series. It was a great triumph, and one that was remembered well into the 1994 season—one that was ultimately cut short by a baseball strike.

Paul Molitor stuck with the Blue Jays for another season before heading over to his home state of Minnesota to play for the Twins. He stayed with the Twins until 1998, when he announced his retirement and the end of his incredible career.

FIVE FUN FACTS

- Paul was a seven time All-Star.
- He had a 39-game hitting streak.
- He was an MVP in 1993.
- At 40 years old, Paul had a .341 batting average.
- He was a first ballot Hall of Fame selection in 2004.

SOME TRIVIA!

How many World Series rings does Molitor have?

Paul Molitor has only one World Series ring.

What was his first year in the Majors?

His first year was 1978.

Does he have a nickname?

They called him "The Ignitor."

When was he inducted into the Hall of Fame?

In 2004.

When did he retire?

Paul Molitor retired in 1998.

REAL-LIFE LESSONS

- Persevere.
- Be a team player.
- Learn from your mistakes.
- Be dedicated.
- Maintain mental clarity.

WADE BOGGS
THE CHICKEN MAN CAN

Wade Boggs was born to Winfield and Sue Boggs on June 15, 1958, in Omaha, Nebraska. He was 11 years of age when his folks picked up and moved to Tampa, Florida, where Wade refined his budding talent for both baseball and football. Wade was a great punter, and many wondered if a career as a professional football player might be in his future.

Once he reached high school, however, he had decided to focus primarily on baseball. He became quite serious about it, too. In fact, he even read entire books on the subject. His dad gave him a book called "The Science of Hitting," authored by none other than baseball batting hero Ted Williams. Wade was determined to become an All-Star slugger just like Ted, and was willing to hunker down and study technique if it helped him improve.

Wade graduated from high school in 1976, which was the same year that he was selected in the 1976 MLB draft. He was drafted in the seventh round, but the fact it took so many rounds didn't bother him, because he had learned that perseverance pays off. He could care less if he was a first or seventh round pick—all that mattered to him was that he was picked.

Wade started out by playing for Minor League teams. Living on a Minor League salary wasn't easy. The money was tight, and Wade later recalled he didn't always have enough money to buy the best food. He found that chicken was the cheapest meat he could buy, so he ate chicken-based meals most of the time.

During this time, he discovered something pretty interesting, He seemed to hit best after he ate chicken. He believed that the protein power of chicken turned him into a power hitter, and he ate chicken religiously for the rest of his baseball career—so much so that he was dubbed the "Chicken Man" by his amused teammates.

At any rate, he battled it out in the Minors for a few years before making his way into the Big Leagues with the Boston Red Sox. He won several batting titles in 1983, and kept his batting average high throughout the rest of the 1980s. Riding high on these stats, made his way into the World Series in 1986.Wade performed well, but his team as a whole came up short, losing to the New York Mets.

Needing a change, Wade made the switch to the New York Yankees in the 1990s and played with the team until 1998. During that time, he kept his batting average well above .300. Wade also went to the World Series with the Yankees in 1996, and his consistent batting helped them come out on top!

FIVE FUN FACTS

- Wade Boggs claims that he once willed himself to be invisible in order to thwart a group of assailants! It sounds utterly absurd, but so far, he's stuck by the story!
- He is a left-handed batter.
- Wade employed what has been called a "slight uppercut swing."
- He loves to fish in his spare time.
- Wade was one of the characters depicted in the famous "The Simpsons" baseball episode "Homer at the Bat."

SOME TRIVIA!

What was Wade's protein power food of choice before a game?

Chicken!

Did Wade have a nickname?

He was known as the Chicken Man.

What unique superstition did Wade have before stepping up to bat?

He would often write the Hebrew word for "life," which in the Latin alphabet translates as "chai." Wade was supposedly caught scratching this word into the dirt on more than one occasion.

How many times was Wade Boggs an All-Star?

He was an All-Star 12 times.

How many World Series rings does he have?

Just one.

REAL-LIFE LESSONS

- Wade always stressed hard work and dedication in the game of baseball and the game of life.
- Don't be afraid to be different. Wade was as unique as they come.
- Have a great sense of humor.
- Be reliable and consistent.
- Be a team player.

LET'S MAKE A BET
ON MOOKIE BETTS

Mookie Betts was born on October 7, 1992, and is part of a new generation of players who are still making major waves in the Major Leagues. His full birth name is actually Markus Lynn Betts, which coincidentally makes his initials *MLB!* Yes, this MLB star, seemingly born with all of the right talents to make him a fabulous hitter, is the literal Mr. MLB!

His parents, Willie and Diana, later remarked that there was never any doubt that their kid would play baseball. As soon as he learned how to walk—and especially when he learned how to run—Mookie was eager to join a team and get right to playing. He grew up in Tennessee, and played for his first team when he and his parents lived in the town of Murfreesboro.

His parents' marriage ended in divorce, but they both still maintained an active role in his life. Even after moving out of the house, his dad still took Mookie back and forth to baseball games.

Mookie kept at it, and soon was enrolled at Overton High School, where he really showed his skills on the baseball field. He was known not only as a good batter, but also a guy who worked well with others on the team. We often hear that it's important to be a team player, and that's true whether on the baseball field or in other aspects of life. Mookie learned this lesson long ago, and knew that it was important to work with others in order to succeed.

After graduating high school, he initially considered college. But after realizing that he already had what it took to play professional baseball, he decided to give it a try. He was drafted by the Boston Red Sox in the fifth round in 2011, and started the 2012 season playing for a Minor League team in the Red Sox farm system called the Lowell Spinners.

He was promoted to the Single-A team Greenville Drive in 2013, and was then placed with the Salem Red Sox that July, where his skill clearly stood out. In 2014, he was bumped up to the Portland Sea Dogs, where he played 54 games before he managed to make it onto a Triple-A team called the Pawtucket Red Sox. Later that summer, he was bumped all the way up to the official Boston Red Sox roster.

He got his start with the Boston Red Sox on June 29, playing an away game against the New York Yankees in Yankee Stadium. That season, Mookie played 52 games and hit five homers, while maintaining a batting average of .291. This was quite impressive for a rookie.

The 2015 season was a good one for the young player, with Mookie upping his home run count to 18. He also hit 42 doubles and 8 triples. While it's the homers that tend to get the most attention, all of those doubles and triples can really drive a team to victory.

Interestingly, his batting average remained around the same, seemingly stuck at .291. It wasn't until the 2016 season that Mookie really began to increase that stat. That year, he bumped his batting average up to .368 and managed to hit 31 home runs and 42 doubles. Mookie and the Sox were triumphant in the AL East Division that season, but were trounced in the 2016 American League Division by the Cleveland Indians.

The 2017 season saw a dip in his fortunes, with his batting average going down to just .264 and his homer count sinking to just 24. Then, in the 2018 season, Mookie took things to another level. That year, he took his team all the way to the top, where he and the Sox managed to beat the LA Dodgers in the World Series.

Mookie ended up being named the American League MVP. He also earned Gold Glove and Silver Slugger awards. It was one heck of a year for the young player!

Interestingly, in 2020, Mookie switched over to the very team he and his Boston buddies had bested in the World Series—the LA Dodgers. This was the year that COVID-19 spread across the planet, leading to a worldwide pandemic. This resulted in an abbreviated and much altered season, due to fears of contagion.

Nevertheless, Mookie led the LA Dodgers to the World Series, where he helped them triumph, just as he had helped his former team, the Boston Red Sox. In doing so, Mookie proved that he was a valuable player who could win the World Series no matter what team he played for.

More importantly, however, he proved that he was a team player. For it wasn't just his own personal skill that led his teams to victory, but also his ability to work with his teammates.

FIVE FUN FACTS

- Mookie is an expert at solving the Rubix Cube!
- He is also an avid bowler.
- Mookie has taken part in two World Series victories.
- He was named after basketball player Mookie Blaylock.
- Rock band Pearl Jam was originally named Mookie Blaylock (in tribute to the basketball star). Mookie Betts was once asked about that, and he responded by stating that he had no clue what Pearl Jam was!

SOME TRIVIA!

When did Mookie first play for the MLB?

In 2004.

How many World Series rings does Mookie have?

He has two.

What is Mookie's favorite food?

He enjoys a good peanut butter and jelly sandwich.

How many teams has Mookie played on?

He's played on two—the Boston Red Sox and the Los Angeles Dodgers.

Does he have a hobby?

Yes! He's an avid bowler.

REAL-LIFE LESSONS

- Work hard.
- Be a team player.
- Keep your focus.
- Have a great sense of humor.
- See the big picture.

PETE ROSE
AND HOW HE GOT HIS HUSTLE

Pete Rose seems to embody everything that's great about baseball. He played and dominated during the mythical era of the Cincinnati Reds known as the "Big Red Machine."

Pete is a native of Cincinnati, having been born there on April 14, 1941. He grew up playing ball, and Cincinnati's Western Hills High School was his proving ground. His baseball coach, a guy known as Pappy Nohr, saw the raw, unrefined talent that Pete brought to the table. He later remarked that he thought Pete had a lot of "grit" and played ball in a clever, strategic manner.

Unfortunately, Pete didn't do quite as well in the classroom. In fact, he flunked out during his sophomore year. In order to not fall behind in his studies, summer school was necessary. But Pete didn't want to cut into summer baseball, so he put himself on what he later jokingly called the "five-year high school plan."

Due to the fact that he was repeating his senior year, he was unable to play for his high school's baseball team during his fifth year at the school. Nevertheless, Pete still found a way to play. He ended up joining the Dayton Amateur League, which was sponsored by the local Frisch's Big Boy restaurant chain.

The real door of opportunity was opened by his Uncle Buddy Bloebaum, who served as a scout for the Cincinnati Reds. Buddy got the Cincinnati Reds to take a look at Pete, and a short time later they signed him to the team. Initially, he was placed with a low-ranking class D baseball team in the Reds' farm system. He played for this team for the 1961 season, and did well enough to receive a "Player of the Year" award.

The following 1962 season was a banner year for Pete, and he was bumped up to the Class A Sally League. There, he gained a reputation for running the bases—even when he was walked! He'd get so excited after a pitcher walked him that he'd run to first base, even though he didn't have to!

Along with his enthusiasm for running to bases, Pete was quickly becoming one of the best batters on the team. His batting average had risen to .330, and he was also a leader in runs, as well as the king of triples (boasting 17 of them that season). With stats like these, Pete seemed destined for the Big Leagues.

He was in spring training in 1963 when he was called to fill in for Reds player Don Blasingame. He then became a regular name on the Reds roster. The fact that he was seen as a replacement for Blasingame (who was subsequently traded to the Washington Senators) created controversy among the team members, some of whom looked at Pete as a sort of unworthy usurper. But if anyone doubted his prowess, Pete was more than ready to make them a believer.

Pete broke out onto the scene with an aggressive and determined streak. He swung hard when at bat and chased balls with vigor while in the outfield. His eagerness was noted by Cincinnati's rivals, the New York Yankees, and it was Yankees players Whitey Ford and Mickey Mantle who began to make sarcastic remarks and calling young Pete "Charlie Hustle."

The nickname stuck, but Pete didn't seem to be fazed by it. He continued to give his all, and made a particularly strong impression on fellow Reds rookie Tommy Harper. According to Harper, Pete was a great source of encouragement. If Harper was ever feeling down, it was Pete who slapped him on the back and encouraged him to keep going.

Pete was eager, but still had a lot to learn, especially when it came to handling veteran players from opposing teams. The wide-eyed young player was actually almost tricked off base in one instance. He had just slid into second base, when the second baseman, who had caught the ball seconds after he was safe, declared that he wanted Pete to step aside for a second so he could dust off the base. Not wanting to offend, Pete very nearly did just that. He was just about to take a step off the base and comply when he realized what was happening—he was about to fall for a prank of the highest order!

After the 1963 season came to a close, Pete enlisted in the United States Army Reserves. This was likely pragmatic thinking on his part, since the Vietnam War wasn't far behind. The United States was already becoming involved in the conflict, and the situation was about to get worse. Back in those days, the draft was still in place, and it was often advantageous for a young man to be enlisted in some form of service, such as the reserves or National Guard, so that they wouldn't be blindsided by a draft notice. This helped them to better control their destiny and where they ended up.

On January 18, 1964, Pete was sent to a basic training camp in Kentucky. He was at Fort Knox for a few months, before being sent over to Fort Thomas. He ended up working as a cook on the base, even though he later claimed that he didn't know how to cook! Ever the quick learner, Rose was soon peeling and frying potatoes with the best of them. The thing he liked best about being a cook was that he was able to get off of his shift early enough to head over to a local ballpark and get in some batting practice.

Pete was definitely trying to avoid being sent to Vietnam, but when he suddenly got a call to head over to Southeast Asia as part of a USO tour, he didn't hesitate. He was a natural performer and entertainer, so this was right up his alley. And to make the deal even sweeter, he was told that his idol, baseball star Joe DiMaggio, would be there with him the whole time. The two athletes took part in a special gig for the troops called the "Major League Baseball Roundup."

Although Joe was retired at this point, Pete had long been a big fan of his. He had admired Joe's performance from afar, and was thrilled to meet him in person. But what stood out to him most was just how nice and humble Joe was. Pete was a bit intimidated to meet such a legend, but Joe made it easy. According to Pete's recollection, Joe was one of the nicest guys he had ever met. He treated Pete with kindness, grace, and good humor.

Pete Rose learned a valuable lesson in all this. It confirmed to him that no matter how big of a star someone might become, they should never lose touch with reality and stop respecting other people.

After his tour of duty was over, Pete made his big return to baseball, becoming one of the best players in the league in the late 1960s and 1970s. During the 1970s in particular, Pete's team became known as the "Big Red Machine." Like a factory churning out tremendous plays, the Reds were extremely productive during this explosive decade of baseball. Pete was right there, helping the team to victory, and in 1976 he led them to a tremendous win in the World Series against the Philadelphia Phillies.

The 1978 season was another great one for Pete, which saw him achieve a 44-game hitting streak. This was Pete's last season with the Reds, and he was happy to leave on a high note.

Pete played for the Philadelphia Phillies from 1979 to 1983, and then had a brief stint with the Montreal Expos in 1984 before he came back to the Reds, finishing up his baseball career with them in 1986.

Ultimately, Pete has always been associated with the Reds, and folks in Cincinnati have always had a soft spot for the energetic initiative of the guy they knew as "Charlie Hustle."

FIVE FUN FACTS

- Pete was nicknamed "Charlie Hustle."
- He served in the Army.
- Pete Rose was friends with Joe DiMaggio.
- He was a switch hitter.
- Pete took part in three World Series victories.

SOME TRIVIA!

When did Pete Rose retire?

He retired in 1986.

How many teams did he play on?

Pete played for three MLB teams—the Reds, Phillies, and Expos.

What was his nickname?

Charlie Hustle!

How many World Series rings does he have?

Three.

What was the name of Pete Rose's Reality TV Show?

Pete Rose: Hits & Mrs.

REAL-LIFE LESSONS

- Always give it your all.
- Stay sharp and focused. Pete Rose always had his eyes on the ball.
- Learn how to read people.
- Stay encouraged and don't lose your enthusiasm.
- Keep a sense of humility. Be kind and gracious to others.

CONCLUSION
THE BEST BATTERS
IN BASEBALL LEARN
THE BEST LESSONS

What do all of the best batters in baseball have in common? Their initiative and determination. Standing in that batter's box, with fast balls whizzing past your face, grit and determination are a necessity—and everyone discussed in this book shared that important attribute.

Ever since Mookie was a rookie, and even before Charlie knew how to hustle, these baseball sluggers were more than ready to make the best of their unique situations.

Of course, baseball has always had a lot of unique characters. Guys like Wade Boggs really take the cake. Wade was known as the Chicken Man on a good day, and claims he became the Invisible Man on a bad day! Meanwhile, Manny Ramirez had similar quirks. Part baseball player, part tricked-out mad scientist, he could hit a home run as easily as he could turn a pair of sunglasses into a stereo system. Baseball just wouldn't be the same without all of these oddballs.

And what about Jose Canseco? He was a home run hero, even though his time in the sport was rather short. He became the "40 40 Man" early in his career, but he faced a lot of challenges as well. Life is a learning process, and great batters like Jose Canseco were keen to learn from their mistakes. Some even wanted to video tape them! At least, Tony Gwynn did. That's how he learned and became a better player—by taping himself at bat and watching his mistakes so he wouldn't repeat them again.

It would be nice if we could all have instant replays of our mistakes in life so that we could learn from them, because at the end of the day, all of the best batters—and the most successful people in every area of life—are life-long learners. They never stop learning and growing, and neither should we!

BONUS SECTION:

Positive Affirmations to Help Young Athletes Improve Confidence and Their Mental Game

1. My confidence is increasing by the day.
2. I shape my own destiny.
3. I lay the foundation of who I am.
4. I'm my number one fan.
5. I accept who I am.
6. I do not shy away from a challenge.
7. I'm focused and determined.
8. Difficult situations only make me better.
9. I'm very talented.
10. I make good choices.
11. I have great courage.
12. I handle challenges with ease.
13. I deserve to be happy.
14. I look forward to the future.
15. Great things are awaiting me.
16. I'm an accomplished baseball player.
17. I love to play ball.
18. I can meet all of my objectives.
19. I have a lot of good things to contribute.
20. I'm an important part of the team.
21. I like who I am.
22. I feel totally at peace.
23. I like to help others.
24. I follow my own course.
25. I know what's best for me.
26. Each day makes me more confident.
27. My outcomes are always positive.
28. I know how to treat others.
29. I train hard.

30. I can bounce back from any difficulty.
31. I know how to stay positive.
32. There is some good in everything.
33. Life is a learning experience.
34. I have love for those around me.
35. I don't mind working on my own.
36. I love what I do.
37. Baseball is fun.
38. I have the right kind of instincts.
39. I always catch the ball.
40. I'll hit a homerun.
41. I'll pitch faster than ever.
42. I'm honest with myself and others.
43. I have integrity.
44. I have an important role to play.
45. I've got a good sense of timing.
46. I inhale calm, and breathe out any worry.
47. I know I'm getting better all the time.
48. My teammates like me.
49. I won't be too hard on myself.
50. I'm clear headed.
51. I'm responsible for my own actions.
52. I let go of anger and embrace empathy.
53. I will help those who are discouraged.
54. My heart is in the right place.
55. I trust my teammates.
56. I welcome constructive criticism.
57. I wish peace to those around me.
58. I respect the opinions of others.
59. I am considerate of my team.
60. My baseball mitt is ready to catch.
61. I feel great as soon as I step to the plate.
62. Life is making me better.
63. I live in the moment.

64. Game day is every day.

65. Everything is coming together.

66. I take it one game at a time.

67. I have everything I need.

68. I take the initiative.

69. I will be positive with every breath.

70. I approve of my development.

71. I strive for excellence.

72. I'm hopeful.

73. I'm eager to try new things.

74. I love to succeed.

75. I'm laser focused.

76. I wear my baseball hat with pride.

77. I have energy to spare.

78. I love solving problems.

79. My teammates are my friends.

80. I wake up ready to go.

81. I feel good.

82. I have self-confidence.

83. I see the best in people.

84. Awesome stuff is headed this way.

85. Baseball keeps me going.

86. I know I'm going to have fun.

87. I have a lot of great advice to give.

88. I'm always on time.

89. I'm secure in who I am.

90. I'm worth it.

91. I'm proud of what I've accomplished.

92. I'm happy with my team.

93. I am entirely fulfilled.

94. I'm getting smarter about baseball.

95. I enjoy being unique.

96. I have everything I need to succeed.

97. We will win the game.

98. I'm confident in the position I play.
99. I contribute a lot to my team.
100. I feel safe and secure.
101. Everything is going to be just fine.
102. All things have a purpose.
103. I'm clever and creative.
104. I'm a hard worker.
105. I will achieve all of my dreams.
106. I'm patient with my teammates.
107. I will follow the rules of the game.
108. I know how to reach my goals.
109. I'm open minded.
110. I am accepting of others.
111. Me and my teammates will do well.
112. I can work with others.
113. The team is getting better every game.
114. I will display good conduct.
115. I appreciate my coach.
116. My teammates appreciate me.
117. I live and let live.
118. I don't hold grudges.
119. I accept the views of others.
120. I'm special as I am.
121. I love and respect others.
122. Life has meaning.
123. I aspire to greatness.
124. I believe in teamwork.
125. My teammates are my friends.
126. We're going to light up the scoreboard.
127. I'm excited about baseball.
128. I treat my teammates well.
129. I keep my mind sharp.
130. I stay physically fit.
131. I make sure to get enough sleep.

132. I eat healthy food.
133. I can't wait to hit home base.
134. I want to contribute to the team.
135. Baseball is my favorite sport.
136. I love to talk to my teammates.
137. I am in control of my life's trajectory.
138. My teammates are all uniquely talented.
139. I learn more each and every day.
140. I'm kind and considerate to others.
141. People like to be around me.
142. I'm a wonderful human being.
143. Everyone has a lot of love to give.
144. I'm competitive but courteous.
145. I've got my eyes on the ball.
146. I know when to swing the bat.
147. I'm ready for anything.
148. It's my time to shine.
149. I forgive others.
150. I like what I see.
151. I speak kindness with every word.
152. Every day is exciting.
153. I have nothing but love for others.
154. I seek clear understanding.
155. I care about my team.
156. I take it as it comes.
157. Every day is new.
158. Baseball invigorates me.
159. I'm compassionate for others.
160. I focus on the good.
161. I respect my elders.
162. It's going to be a good day.
163. We're going to have fun.
164. I have good health.
165. My needs are fulfilled.

166. My teammates are supportive
167. I'm ready to play ball.
168. I'll make the audience go wild.
169. There is nothing I lack.
170. I'm prosperous.
171. Opportunity awaits.
172. My dreams will become reality.
173. Life is a gift.
174. I'm a positive influence.
175. My game keeps getting better.
176. I love the baseball diamond.
177. I'm not easily dismayed.
178. Me and my teammates really gel.
179. I know how to have fun.
180. I give voice to my opinions.
181. I know how to make compromises.
182. I can see things from multiple views.
183. I have a whole lot of resources.
184. I'm hopeful for the future.
185. I am grateful.
186. I keep everything well maintained.
187. My skills are finely honed.
188. I've got my cleats on.
189. I am open and honest with others.
190. I openly share my talents and abilities.
191. I'm a responsible member of the team.
192. I'm happy for others who succeed.
193. I exercise self-control.
194. I am full of energy and ambition.
195. Each moment is a blessing.
196. Every second counts.
197. I practice good health.
198. I'm in perfect shape.
199. Regular training makes me great.

200. I'm healthier than ever.
201. I feel great.
202. I am prepped and ready to play.
203. I'm a base running machine!
204. Nothing is too difficult.
205. The bat feels good in my hands.
206. I have full control of the ball.
207. My attention is focused.
208. I listen to my own body.
209. I stay well-nourished and fit.
210. My mental wellbeing is good.
211. I'm a skilled member of the team.
212. People love what I bring to the game.
213. Great days are ahead.
214. Baseball is what I do.
215. I have a lot to offer.
216. I'm still learning new things.
217. I will do what's right.
218. I'm a problem solver.
219. I work well with my team.
220. I'm up for it.
221. Victory is on the horizon.
222. I crave good health.
223. I'm always looking for fun.
224. I'm steady and confident.
225. I don't complain.
226. I'm ready to make adjustments.
227. My performance is up to par.
228. There are things I can teach others.
229. I am more than enough.
230. I want to be a good example to my team.
231. Baseball makes me feel fulfilled.
232. I have plenty of room to grow.
233. I keep my attention focused.

234. I'm making the world a better place.
235. I love what I do.
236. I'm going to succeed.
237. I feel inspired.
238. I know I'm going to do well.
239. I'm going to make a difference.
240. The team is going to be successful.
241. I make a great contribution to the team.
242. Baseball is a gift.
243. Errors make baseball more meaningful.
244. Baseball only gets better.
245. I'm living the dream.
246. I wake up refreshed.
247. Baseball is my buddy.
248. I look on the bright side of baseball.
249. I'm going to send that ball flying!
250. I have value and worth.
251. My coach likes what I do.
252. My teammates appreciate me.
253. I keep finding new opportunities.
254. I have great enthusiasm.
255. I have a good work ethic.
256. I'm at peace with myself.
257. I always have a positive word.
258. I think well of others.
259. My hard work will be rewarded.
260. I'm in a good place in life.
261. My heart leads the way.
262. I am loved for my uniqueness.
263. I care for others.
264. I have plenty to give.
265. I make all the right choices.
266. There's always something good in store.
267. I believe in optimism.

268. I freely praise others.
269. I want to listen and learn from others.
270. There's a lot of great insight to be had.
271. I treat others well.
272. I'm motivated to play ball.
273. It's going to be a great game.
274. I'm proactive.
275. I'm very detail oriented.
276. I can navigate through life's challenges.
277. I am happy with who I am.
278. I will allow myself to be glad.
279. I'm going to be productive.
280. My team will do well.
281. I'm excited about life.
282. I'm going to stay on track.
283. I will make it to the finish line.
284. I am very insightful.
285. I have faith in my team.
286. My teammates are supportive.
287. We can achieve our dreams.
288. I have the right mental mindset.
289. I have compassion for others.
290. I always do my best.
291. I learn from hardship.
292. I find unique ways to succeed.
293. I can throw a fast ball like no other.
294. I always hit the ball.
295. I feel motivated.
296. I won't give up.
297. We're in it to win it.
298. I will reach my goals.
299. I choose to be happy.
300. I'm relaxed and at peace.
301. Every moment is a joy.

302. I won't get overwhelmed.
303. I wake up excited to do well.
304. I make my own happiness.
305. I know how to win.
306. Baseball makes me smile.
307. I will work hard.
308. I will make life meaningful.
309. I'm receptive to feedback.
310. I have good things to offer.
311. I'm in tune with my emotions.
312. I take time to enjoy the simple things.
313. I uplift myself and others.
314. I have great initiative.
315. My goals are within reach.
316. I will stay on task.
317. I cherish memorable moments.
318. I love being part of the team.
319. I'm not easily shaken.
320. I'm strong.
321. I have the right mentality to succeed.
322. I take charge of my own happiness.
323. I look forward to a great game.
324. No room for worry—only happiness.
325. My body is relaxed—my mind is focused.
326. I embrace peaceful thoughts.
327. I know how to plan ahead.
328. Every inning counts.
329. We're going to run the bases.
330. I'll pitch a perfect game.
331. We will never get struck out.
332. My team's unbeatable.
333. I have what it takes.

THE MENTAL MINDSET TO HELP YOU SUCCEED IN BASEBALL

In baseball you have to be competitive. A competitive mindset is important as it pertains to doing well in the sport. Nevertheless, young players need to also learn how to handle setbacks when they come their way. It takes a certain mindset to be able to succeed in baseball. Let's learn more about how we can best develop that mind set.

AFFIRMATIONS

The first step to developing a positive mindset is to make sure that you believe in yourself. Positive affirmations as presented earlier in this book, are a great way to reinforce your own sense of self-confidence. These affirmations do not necessarily have to be spoken aloud. But it would be helpful to have them written down somewhere so that you can silently read them as a source of encouragement. You can write them in a notebook, or even on some other item you happen to use frequently. Manny Ramirez for example, was famous for scribbling positive affirmations on the bottom of his shoes! Just like Manny, find a way to remind yourself of all of the good things that you've got going for you.

FACE YOUR EMOTIONS

We all have emotions. We express joy, sadness, and frustration through our emotions. If a baseball player knocks a ball out of the park, we see their emotional excitement on full display, as they run the bases. There is nothing wrong with feeling emotion, but we need to have a good handle on how to express these emotions. For if we let our emotions get too out of control, they can become a hindrance far more than a help. Emotions shouldn't be suppressed, but we also shouldn't be consumed by them. We need to face our emotions and express them in a reasonable manner.

SET GOALS

In order to keep your mind focused, we need to set goals for ourselves. Goals help us see our progress in real time as we achieve greater and even more impressive objectives. Nothing boosts the confidence more than a job well done.

BE A TEAM PLAYER

Sports require team effort and baseball is certainly no different. You need to have the mindset of a team player. It's important to learn how to cooperate with your teammates. Even if you haven't yet played for a team, you can learn how to cooperate with family and friends. If you can get along with them, then you are better prepared to cooperate with your baseball teammates as well.

ACKNOWLEDGE THERE IS ALWAYS MORE TO LEARN

Baseball—like life—is a learning process. We need to therefore develop the mindset of a learner. Don't approach baseball like an absolute expert. Take things as they come and be ready to learn as you go. Be willing to learn and better refine your techniques as you play the game. Also, be open to criticism and always try to learn from any errors you may make.

THE TEAMS

Baseball consists of two teams playing against each other in the baseball diamond. One team is on the offense trying to score points, while the other is on the defense trying to get the other team out. It's called a baseball diamond because of the shape that the bases make. Counting counterclockwise from 1st—you have 1st base, 2nd base, 3rd base, and then the home plate. The offensive team positions their batters at home plate as the defensive team pitches the ball. If the batter hits the ball, they can run the bases. Depending on where the ball goes, catchers in the outfield try to throw the ball to the bases the batter tries to run to. The defensive team has players stationed at every base, as well as shortstop and the pitcher's mound. These players coordinate with each other to try to throw the ball to the base before the batter can get there. If the batter is running to first for example and the first baseman catches it before the batter can touch down on the base—that batter is out. After three outs, the teams switch and the defensive team goes on offense and is at bat.

EQUIPMENT

Basic baseball gear consists of baseball mitts, bats, baseballs, and uniforms. Baseball cleats and protective batting helmets are also typical gear for baseball.

PLAYING BASICS

There are nine innings in a baseball game. Each inning features one team at bat, and the other team in defensive positions on the field. The defensive team's pitcher stands at the pitcher's mound right in front of homebase. The pitcher can pitch the ball straight through what's referred to as the "strike zone." Any pitch within this zone is a fair ball that the batter can hit. The pitcher however, might throw a curve ball that goes too far to the right or left to be considered within the strike zone. The batter has the right to simply let these balls fly past them. Doing so, allows them to be granted a "ball." If they rack up four balls—they are then allowed to walk to first base. If the batter however, does not swing and the ball is within the strike zone and considered fair—it's considered a strike. If they get three strikes—they are out. Three outs and the teams switch places on the field.

RULES TO KEEP IN MIND

Baseball is an enjoyable sport to play, but it's a game that consists of rules. In order to have a successful mindset playing it therefore—we need to keep those rules front and center in our mind.

Some specific rules to consider are:

- 3 strikes is an out.
- 4 balls let's you walk.
- 3 outs end an inning.
- Out of bound (fall) balls are not counted.

Made in the USA
Columbia, SC
09 December 2024

48747814R00070